LORD
KNOWS
THIS SH*T
AIN'T EASY

LORD KNOWS THIS SH*T AIN'T EASY

How to Stay Emotionally Balanced in a CHAOTIC WORLD

....

ADELFA MARR

Hierophantpublishing

Cover design by Laura Beers
Print book interior design by Frame25 Productions

Hierophant Publishing
San Antonio, Texas
www.hierophantpublishing.com

If you are unable to order this book from your local bookseller,
you may order directly from the publisher.

Library of Congress Control Number: 2023900501

ISBN: 978-1-950253-37-1

10 9 8 7 6 5 4 3 2 1

To Umi, Manny, Mami, Papi & Nads.
And my spirit team, of course.

Contents

Foreword

Reader, watch out!

The book you hold in your hands is nothing short of dynamite. If you're not ready to level up, change your life, and discover a brave new version of yourself, I suggest you back away slowly.

Actually, scratch that. Stay right there, because you *are* ready. If you've picked up this book, then life is already whispering in your ear and tugging at your sleeve. It's telling you that the time has come to take the next step toward wholeness. And luckily for you, Adelfa Marr is the perfect person to show you the way.

Hanging out with Adelfa in any form—whether in person, online, or in print—is like stepping into a warm pool of sunlight. She has a gift of kindness that makes you feel safe and empowered to take the big leaps you've been putting off and face the fears that have been gnawing at your mind and heart.

In my own inner work, as well as in my professional roles as workshop facilitator and author of the *Warrior Goddess Training* series, I have found that one of the biggest struggles for most people today is releasing the habitual "need to control." In *Lord Knows This Sh*t Ain't Easy*, Adelfa shows you that your true power lies in giving up control, and your true strength lies in trusting that you are strong, and flexible, and courageous enough to take life as it comes. Her wisdom and sense of humor will convince even the most die-hard control freaks that life gets better when you let go.

Of course, it's not surprising that we find ourselves in this dilemma. From a very early age, most of us are taught that we can control our appearance, our relationships, our personalities, our careers, and the outcomes of almost every situation if we only try hard enough. When our attempts to control all these things don't work, we often blame ourselves. But really, life was never ours to control in the first place.

When you're holding a hammer, everything looks like a nail. And when the hammer you're holding is control, life becomes a never-ending attempt to pound things into the form you think they should take, eliminating anything unwanted or unexpected. The problem is that, when you knock out these "undesirable" aspects of life, you eliminate life's magic as well.

When you funnel a wild stream into an underground culvert, you may have less surface flooding to deal with, but you also lose the beauty and vitality of the stream. Likewise, when you suppress "undesirable" emotions, you miss out on the beauty and vitality that is released by feeling them completely. And when you avoid "undesirable" moments in life, you miss out on the growth that is waiting for you just on the other side of the discomfort.

When you wake up to the fact that control is not only impossible, but also not the answer, life takes on new depth and meaning. I find that life is always unfolding for my benefit, even when it may not seem that way.

Adelfa is attuned to these facts because she's lived them. Like many of us, she spent years putting up inner walls and suppressing her emotions, only to wonder why life didn't get any easier. In *Lord Knows This Sh*t Ain't Easy*, she shares the tools she discovered for relinquishing her iron grip on control and starting down a path of self-awareness, courageous authenticity, and resilient responsiveness to life. She has used these tools to help countless clients live their best lives and now she makes them available to you as well.

So here's to you for picking up this book, and for taking the first step toward finding emotional balance in this messy, uncertain, surprising, and utterly magical world of ours. May your heart be as wide as the ocean, and your soul as free as the wind. And may you trust that life is giving you what you need to grow. You don't need to control it.

—HeatherAsh Amara

Chapter 1

Stop Trying to Control Sh*t

Living in the world today is no joke. Don't get me wrong. I'm not some nostalgic "life used to be better" person. I know inhabiting a body as a conscious being has never been easy. But this moment in history is a doozy. After all, if you're reading this, you've survived a global pandemic, along with all the challenges it brought to our relationships, our working conditions, and even our basic existence. Life in the 21st century has already had its share of uncertainty, anxiety, and downright terror. We can no longer count on finding our favorite bread at the grocery store, let alone finding love or landing our dream job.

Trying to stay emotionally balanced amid all this chaos is like being on a runaway horse with no saddle—and the state of the world makes it feel as if the horse is heading straight to the edge of a gloomy forest. For most of my own life, even before the challenges of the last few years, keeping emotional balance meant staying in control. In my mind, being in control of my emotions—and ideally, the emotions of everyone around me—was the only thing that could keep me safe, in the know, and ready for all the "what ifs" in life. As a result, I rehearsed all potential conversations. I imagined every possible scenario I might encounter on a given day, planning my responses to every interaction and my reactions to every trigger. I truly believed that I could eliminate any uncertainty, awkwardness, or discomfort from my life if I just thought hard enough.

This pursuit of control kept my relationships in tidy little boxes, with no room for messiness, conflict, or true intimacy. I swore I could only be safe if I was in control, so control was always my goal. You can imagine how much fun it was to be around me. What I called "safety" looked more like rigidity, paranoia, and insecurity. I had no boundaries, and I compulsively filled the wants and needs of those around me regardless of how much it cost me in terms of time, energy, or emotional exhaustion. I was so focused on what other people were thinking and feeling that I couldn't identify my own real intentions or desires. My life force was tied up in the project of controling others' perceptions of me—an exhausting and depressing way to live.

The only thing keeping me from being a total and utter jerk was the fact that my need for control was rooted in good intentions. I wasn't a cartoon villain seeking world domination. I wanted to remain in control because I had this dire need to be ready for whatever life threw my way—the good, the bad, and the ugly. I also cared so much about other people that I considered it my personal responsibility to make sure they were never sad, bored, uncomfortable, or disappointed, even for a split second. I assumed every expression that flickered across someone's face had something to do with me, and I felt a sense of panic and failure if a friend or even a total stranger showed a hint of negative emotion when in my presence.

In my quest for total "readiness," I had lost touch with a basic fact: *I was terrified*. Terrified of being caught in a social situation—shit, any situation—without knowing what to say. Terrified of revealing an emotion I hadn't intended to feel in the first place. Terrified of making some tiny slip-up that would cause my entire life to unravel. Terrified that people wouldn't like me, and that their normal experiences of stress, disappointment, irritation, and boredom were somehow my fault. Terrified that my job in the universe was to make everything right for all people at all times, and that there would be horrendous consequences if I didn't. I thought that, if I could only rehearse a perfect, likeable, interesting self, I could somehow control how other people saw me, and therefore how they felt.

It sounds silly now, but I honestly thought I needed to be in charge of everyone else's eyes, ears, and hearts. I mean, what would happen if I didn't play out every conversation in my head before it took place in real life? How could I be sure the right words would leave my mouth and the right emotions would show on my face? How could I be sure my body language would convey the blend of kindness, sympathy, and enthusiasm guaranteed to make others feel wonderful? Would people still like me if I didn't deliver the five-star experience they surely expected from me at all times? And how could I handle the anxiety I would feel if I failed to lift their mood, or solve their problems, or right their wrongs?

I was trapped by these fears and insecurities. I didn't feel good about myself, and I convinced myself that the reason was that I wasn't skilled enough at controlling my own emotions and the emotions of everyone around me. Then one day it hit me . . .

Houston, we have a problem.

Mission Control

It's me, Houston. I'm the problem. My need to maintain minute control over how other people saw me had forced me into a mindset in which I could barely feel my own emotions. I was keenly aware of small fluctuations in others' moods—"Oh no, they're getting tired!" "No, wait, they're disappointed because I haven't said or done the right thing!" The problem was that I was not placing equal importance on my own feelings—maybe *I* was tired! Maybe *I* was feeling let down by something *they'd* failed to do! Instead of experiencing my emotions, I was managing them like employees, expecting them to show up on time and do the tasks they were assigned. Somehow, this strategy had persisted all the way into my twenties, but now it was starting to break down.

Let me back up a little and explain. I'm a born-and-bred New Yorker, the child of immigrant parents who worked extremely hard and were willing to give you their last dime. My story isn't new. I was one of millions of brown girls growing up in the projects and living a wonderful life. I might not have described it as wonderful then, but I can look back at my younger years now and see that I was *truly* blessed. Like everyone, I had hurdles to overcome and expectations to meet, but I also had ample opportunities and was surrounded by love. And, like everyone else, I'd developed my fair share of not-so-helpful survival strategies in response to the normal challenges of life—people-pleasing, an intense preoccupation with what others thought of me, the desire to be seen as perfect in every social situation, and a deep need for control.

I can now see that fear was at the root of these unhelpful habits. Fear that I wasn't good enough. Fear that others wouldn't like me and that I would experience some

uncomfortable emotions as a result. Rather than looking within and dealing with these fears, I kept sweeping
them under the rug and pretending they weren't there.
After all, my survival strategies had done a pretty good
job of protecting me so far. So what if they left me feeling drained, unfulfilled, and small?

As you have likely experienced yourself, life has a
way of pushing us out of our comfort zones when we
need to grow. In my case, life presented me with a new
opportunity. My partner invited me to relocate with him
to Southern California, and it felt like walking onto a
movie set—clear blue skies atop sparkling oceans, stun-
ning people walking around, and spectacular weather
every day. It seemed as if everyone I met was doing something worth writing home about. Everyone except me,
that is.

Once outside my familiar comfort zone of New York,
I crumpled. I didn't know where I fit in this new environment, or who I was supposed to be. In New York, I'd
never had to face these questions, but now they jumped
out at me from every corner. I worried that I was the
wrong kind of person for California, or the wrong kind
of person, period. It didn't take long for me to fall into
a depressive rut. Having taken this big leap to the West
Coast, I was flooded with anxiety that I would never
amount to anything, that I would be a disappointment

to my parents and friends back home, and that I would let down my partner.

To make things worse, I felt guilty, because, after all, my life was great in many ways. And yet there I was, battling anxiety attacks so intense that they made me pass out at least once a week. My friends, my family, and my partner started to worry about me. *I* started to worry about me. It was clear that things were out of alignment in a big way. Just because everything was beautiful in my external reality didn't mean that I was okay on the inside. In fact, the more picture-perfect my life became, the more painfully I felt the gap between my sunny external reality and my dark and stormy insides.

I started seeing a therapist to work out my kinks. I realized that I felt hideous within my own self, and that my now-husband had no business being with someone as ordinary as I was. But while my journey in therapy yielded many benefits, I still didn't feel as if I had the answers I wanted. I had better tools to manage my anxiety, but I was still yearning for a deeper understanding of myself. Once I was out of immediate crisis, I could feel a door opening inside me. I sensed a new place begging to be explored. And I heard a small inner voice beckoning me forward.

But I knew this was a place I had to explore alone—not because I didn't need others or didn't get inspired by others, but because this was *my* journey to take. To do this work, I had to dig into myself and find the roots of what was going on inside me. Then I had to find new ways to grow, to branch out, and to blossom.

As part of my exploration process, I started to question everything. Who am I? What do I stand for? What do I expect of myself? I couldn't continue to base my own self-image on what other people expected of me. Not what my parents wanted, even though they had lived their entire lives so I would have the opportunity to become the success they dreamed of. Not what my friends wanted, even if they imagined only the best for me. I had to discover who I was outside of my conditioning. And most importantly, I had to answer two questions: What now? What next?

I began to wonder what it would be like if I asked myself whether *I* was okay before worrying about whether others were okay. What would it be like if I didn't assume I had to fix everything that didn't feel perfect? Once I started down this line of inquiry, I kept going further and further. What if I put my energy, effort, and time into the one person who had always wanted it, needed it, and yearned for it? Me! What if I started living for myself in the same way I'd always lived for others? When I experimented with this approach, I discovered that it felt really nice. Granted, I didn't have much practice at living this way. Sometimes it felt awkward. It was uncomfortable for me to acknowledge my own feelings, and I worried that I was being selfish if I so much as identified my own wants and needs. And I still reverted to my old way of doing things when I felt overwhelmed.

My vision had always been 20/20 when it came to the things I *didn't* want, but now I was gaining clarity about the things I *did* want. I wanted a life in which I was responsible for my own feelings first—a life in which I could see someone else's imperfections and not feel that I had to put on my cape and swoop in to save the day. I needed to come back to *myself*. I needed to relearn how to live for myself—how to find balance between my own emotions and the care I have for the emotions of others. And I had to do this in a world that felt insane and chaotic—a world that was clearly in need of saving.

I spent a lot of time imagining the person I *wanted* to be: a strong, confident, happy person. Someone who could set a boundary without falling prey to spiraling anxieties about it for the next three months. Someone who could share an opinion or state a position without worrying about how it would be received. Someone who could live without the constant fear of displeasing others. The more I envisioned this confident, self-aware person, the more excited I became about becoming her—and the more strongly I resolved that I would no longer let my insecurities run my life.

I threw my entire being into this project. I went back to therapy. I devoured every self-help book I could get my hands on. I talked about personal growth to anyone who would listen. I discovered communities on social media where others were sharing their own stories of transformation—and I was hooked. Slowly but surely, I gave up my obsession with control and began to trust that I could handle whatever came up, whether I had "prepared" for it or not. I stopped taking on impossible tasks that had never been my responsibility to begin with. I began to experience my emotions as powerful messengers giving me important information about my life. I started to see them as allies, instead of enemies.

I started my coaching practice with one goal in mind—to help people find emotional balance. Using my personal experience of overcoming crippling anxiety, I devoted my practice to helping others give up their toxic relationship with control and step into a life of spontaneity, ease, and purpose. Since then, I've worked with individuals from all walks of life, both in private sessions and in online healing circles where people come together to share their journeys. I hope that this book will function as a healing circle you can take with you anywhere—a companion on your own path toward wholeness.

The Challenge

When was the last time you were out in the world as the *real* you? Not the version you think will make others happy, but the one that fills your own cup? When was the last time you told someone how you *really* felt, without worrying about what they'd think or how they'd react? When was the last time you let yourself feel your own emotions fully, without trying to edit them, distract yourself from them, or replace them with "better" ones? When was the last time you stepped out of your comfort zone and reached for the kind of life you actually want?

In this book, I want to challenge you to do exactly that. But don't worry—you don't have to do it alone. I'll be there every step of the way, sharing my favorite tools for building your confidence, helping you grow out of old patterns, and working with you to develop a trusting and joyful relationship with the unknown. This book will teach you how to:

* Get in touch with your own feelings and desires, and find your right relationship to others' needs and perceptions.

* Stop fearing the inevitable moments when somebody may dislike you, or unfriend you, or read you the wrong way.

* Experience your emotions and even appreciate them, not simply endure them or spend large amounts of energy trying to control them.

* Free up energy that is currently going into these "control" tasks so you can use it to make

your own life more joyful and work for positive change in the larger world

* Replace controlling behaviors with trust, spontaneity, and ease.

Staying emotionally balanced is what allows us to be helpful to ourselves and others. It's what makes us more effective in finding solutions to challenging situations. It provides a restful island of peace in the stormy seas of chaos. It's hard. It takes a lot of practice. And you have to be willing to fall on your face as you try. But the better you get at cultivating emotional balance, the better you fare in even the most stressful situations. The result is far less suffering in your own life and in the lives of those you love.

I spent so many years in mental chaos and emotional instability. I was a worrywart and a control freak. If that's where you are right now, know that you're not alone. I get it. You may not believe it yet, but everyone can move into a life they want and a life they love. This book will take you step by step through practices that can help you make these changes. I'll share stories from my own life, as well as those of my clients that have left deep imprints in my heart and impacted my own healing journey. Each chapter is full of strategies you can try, practices you can play with, and attitudes you can dance with. Many chapters contain questions and prompts that I encourage you to journal about, dream about, and discuss with loved ones who are on their own healing paths.

And most of all, remember that this is *your* journey. I'm aware that some of what I share here may not move you. When you find yourself in that moment, don't fret. Just because a part of what I share doesn't speak to you, that does not mean the rest of the book won't. Take what resonates for you and leave the rest. That said, I also want to push you to go beyond just reading. I don't want you to stay up in your head and *think* about what you read here: the goal is to live it. This is a heart journey. Healing is a physical process. Bringing your whole self to the table is what will make this journey really juicy. I hope you can find grace for yourself in the times you fumble and celebrate yourself for every time you realize that you are a little better than you were the day before.

I hope this book will serve as a companion, a guide, an understanding friend, and a safe space for you to discover the life that feels right for you. Because, at the end of the day, we're all in this together. And lord knows, this shit ain't easy.

Chapter 2

How to Observe Sh*t and Why

I remember the day I got this text from my dad: "Mom's in the hospital, in the ICU. It's not looking good."

What? No, really. What the hell? I had spoken to my mom that morning, as I do each day. She'd sounded like her normal, cheerful self, checking in on her grandkid and reminding me to eat. She hadn't mentioned feeling sick. In fact, she'd told me she was planning to go grocery shopping with my dad after they got the laundry done. How did the day shift from a shared to-do list to an admission to the intensive care unit?

As I absorbed the news of my mom's impending death, the world went into slow motion. Horrifying scenarios began to scroll through my head, and my whole body began to tingle as if it were going numb. I could hear birds chirping outside the window of my office—I'd just finished an online coaching session with a client— but the sound seemed to belong to an entirely different universe than the one I was inhabiting. How could I live without my mom? How could my baby son grow up without his grandma? How could I face a single morning without hearing her voice on the phone? It felt as if my world were shattering, the pieces exploding apart, never to be put back together again.

I called my dad. Muffled behind tears and soft sobs, he told me Mom was in the ICU, intubated, and that no one knew what had happened. "It came out of nowhere," he told me. I hung up and began to scream.

Literally scream. I paced the floor, stopped to belt out a guttural yell, then started pacing again. My body surged with fear and panic. I felt like a fish pulled out of the water, flopping around and desperately trying to breathe. All I wanted was to be back in the water—to have my reality go back to the way it had been before I got my father's text. But amid my screams and cries, a thought cut through my mind with total clarity: "You are wylin' right now."

Hold up. Who said that? Was there somebody else there, a second Adelfa who *wasn't* caught in spooked mode? Who was, in fact, watching everything calmly? How could I be both panicking and gently steering myself away from panic *at the same time*?

I slowed down my pacing and waited for this other Adelfa to speak again.

"That's good," she said. "Take a breath. Now, what you're going to do is pick up your phone and call your husband."

Thanks to this other Adelfa's calm encouragement, I was able to carry out this simple task. I picked up my phone and called my husband, who showed up in less than five minutes. Holding my hyperventilating body tightly, he called my dad. When he asked my dad to explain what was going on, he learned that it was *my dad's* mom who was in the hospital. My own mom was fine. She had not gotten into a freak accident. In fact, she was on her way to the hospital to visit my ninety-six-year-old grandma right now.

As I absorbed the news that my mom was okay, my heart rate began to slow down. I found myself attempting to hold space for the real panic I had felt, as well as the wave of sadness for my grandmother that was now cresting over me. I began to think of ways I could support my dad through this difficult time. I was amazed and a little sheepish at how quickly my mind had given in to panic, bolting ahead of the present moment into disasters that hadn't even happened.

From Wylin' to Observing

When I heard that inner voice telling me I was wylin', I slipped into what I now call "observer mode." Suddenly, it was as if I could see myself from a distance. I wasn't in *control* of my emotions, exactly, but they felt separate from me, like images playing across a screen. I couldn't control my physical reactions, either—my palms were still sweating and my heart was still fluttery—but the overriding panic was draining away. Instead of getting swept up in these reactions, my brain was giving me commentary that was factual and grounding. After going through a lifetime of emotions in less than an hour, I was amazed at how clear and calm I was starting to feel. I had a hunch that, if I worked with my inner observer and made it stronger, I wouldn't need to wyle out so much the next time my dad fat-fingered his phone.

Observation is key to finding and maintaining emotional balance, because until you are aware of what's happening in your body and mind, especially in times of stress, you will continue to be reactive—fighting the storms of life, wasting a great deal of energy, and surrendering your inner power in the process. The mere act of observing yourself creates some distance between you and your mental and physical reactions. It's like watching a pack of wild animals in a nature documentary, instead of letting those same animals loose in your living room. Developing your powers of observation helps you to feel safe and grounded, instead of constantly on edge. It helps you make good decisions, instead of acting out of fear. And if you're stuck in old habits, observation helps you identify what they are so you can move into new patterns.

If I'd been firmly established in observer mode when I got that text from my dad, I could have stayed on the phone with him long enough to figure out what was actually going on, instead of immediately hanging up and panicking. I could have told myself to gather some more information before going too far down this rabbit hole. I could have resolved the entire situation within a few seconds, instead of pacing around my office like a crazy person, living out one of my biggest fears through screaming and yelling until my throat was sore. I could have watched my panic coming up, and said: "OK, panic, I see you. But hold up a minute. I want to check on a few things before I let you in."

When you don't know how to activate your observer mode, you can make all sorts of mistakes and cause all sorts of unnecessary chaos. Who hasn't made a bad decision when overwhelmed by panic or misplaced anger, only to spend weeks or months mopping up the damage? I mean, we've all engaged in social media rants that we look back on two hours later, cringing with our entire bodies. And we've all had instances of jumping into action before getting all the facts.

Sometimes it can feel as if your emotions are running *you*, instead of the other way around. Instead of feeling your emotions, you react to them, and this keeps you in a constant state of emergency in which you can cause problems for yourself and others. When you switch to observer mode, your emotions stop bossing you around, and you reclaim your ability to take appropriate action.

You realize that emotions are *not* a threat, but merely signals to which you can respond in whatever way you see fit.

Your Inner Doorbell Camera

When my friend's partner got a new job, they had to move from their quiet mountain homestead to an apartment in downtown San Francisco. My friend had never lived in a big city before, but now her front door opened onto a busy shopping street. Total strangers often sat on her stoop at night, eating burritos from the taqueria next door. Every now and then, an Amazon package was stolen, or a drunk guy cozied up in their doorway for the night. My friend sometimes lay awake, wondering who was out there and freaking out about the proximity of so many human lives. Sometimes the people on her doorstep were so noisy it almost sounded as if they'd made their way inside.

After they'd been living there for a month, my friend's partner installed a smart doorbell camera to keep an eye on the apartment's entrance. Now they can easily check who is out there without the risk of opening the door. My friend's anxiety began to diminish when she watched footage from the camera and realized that most of the people who showed up there were perfectly harmless, if sometimes obnoxious. Sure, she might not *like* the fact that a drunk guy was sleeping on her doorstep, but at least now she could see that it wasn't harming her in any way. There was no need to spring into action and *do* anything about it. Keeping an eye on it—*observing* it—was enough.

This kind of doorbell camera is the ultimate observer. It just sits there, dutifully watching everyone who comes up to the door—the hot UPS guy, the mean-looking Amazon lady, the noisy burrito eaters, the mentally disturbed man who wanders by in the night to leave cans of string beans on the door mat for no apparent reason. It doesn't react to any of these visitors; it just keeps an eye on them, recording their behavior in detail. At the same time, it provides valuable information and answers important questions. Who's hanging around my house? Are they friends or enemies? Do I need to be afraid of them, or can I be chill? How big a threat is the string-bean man, really?

My friend's doorbell camera helped her feel more comfortable as she adjusted to crowded city life. It helped her understand that, although plenty of people came to the door, she didn't have to let them inside. She could see that there was a predictable pattern to these visits, and she didn't need to be on edge all the time. Over time, she also realized that non-action was usually the best choice. There was no point in trying to control the scene at her doorstep. Like a self-contained ecosystem, it more or less controlled itself. The drunk guy always wandered away eventually. The burrito eaters left their wrappers behind—which was certainly rude of them— but it was easier to toss the wrappers in the trash than to try to change their behavior. If my friend saw something serious happening, like a fight or a mugging, she could always call the police. But most things fell into the "not serious" category, and she could reclaim her inner peace by simply letting them pass.

Up Your Curiosity; Drop Your Judgment

Don't get me wrong. Observing yourself can be scary as hell. You're going to see things that make you uncomfortable. In some moments, you may even find yourself saying: "Wait, this is the whole reason I *don't* want an inner doorbell camera!" We all have feelings we'd rather avoid, thoughts we'd rather suppress, and patterns we'd rather not see. That's why it's important that, when you start paying attention to these things, you do so with a spirit of curiosity rather than judgment.

Moving from judgment to curiosity is a huge shift. After all, doesn't some level of judgment keep us safe, or stop us from being bad people? The problem arises when we treat our thoughts and feelings like threats—something to be controlled or even eliminated. When we tell ourselves: "Oh, don't feel jealous of her. That's wrong; you should feel happy for her." Or: "Don't have *that* thought! If you were a good person, you'd be having *this* thought instead." But our thoughts and feelings are rarely under our control. Even though we experience them as internal phenomena, it's more helpful to think of them as external conditions, like the weather, the chirping of birds, or the traffic on the road.

We wouldn't beat ourselves up for not having control over the weather, the traffic, or the birds—yet we judge ourselves over and over for not being able to control our thoughts and emotions. We assume that, because they seem to be happening inside our minds and bodies, they "must" be something we can control, but this couldn't be further from the truth. Like the clouds in the sky, thoughts and emotions arise out of a complex interplay of factors: our environment, our culture, our memories, the state of our bodies, the state of our communities and families, and so on. They're not *meant* to be changed or controlled; they're meant to be experienced calmly and without judgment. And if we do long to have more positive thoughts and emotions, the first step to achieving that is always accepting the thoughts and emotions we already have.

In my case, I approached observation as if I were a stranger interested in getting to know me—minus my habitual worry that this stranger would soon discover something terrible about me and hate me. Getting into this mindset was not an easy task, especially for a control freak like me. Like many people, I was afraid that, if I looked deeply at my innermost self, I wouldn't like what I found. I had to practice being curious. I had to ask questions like: "Why does this person feel so nervous right now?" Or: "That's interesting, her instinct is to avoid conflict. I wonder where that came from?"

This observation process can be quite humbling. Don't get me wrong—it's *hard* to watch unexpected or unwanted emotions flare up and take over your body and mind. But no matter what comes up, it's extremely important to be honest with all you're experiencing, thinking, and feeling. In fact, if you're not being honest about what you're observing—whether that's because you prefer what you "should" feel over what you actually feel, or because your observations bring up discomfort about the state of your life and yourself—you can't begin to make adjustments. It's only when you're honest about your observations that you can acknowledge your true starting point.

Take Inventory

Spend some time reviewing the footage of your inner doorbell camera. Which emotions come up for you on a regular basis? How do you typically react to each one? For example, a client of mine noticed that, whenever she felt a sense of uncertainty about a project she was working on, she unconsciously reacted to the uncertainty by getting up and making a cup of tea. By the end of the workday, she was wired on caffeine! Another client realized that, when she felt irritated with someone, she tried to talk herself out of it by thinking about all the reasons she ought to be compassionate toward that person. She didn't want to see or experience her own capacity for irritation, so she tried to fast-forward through that part of the tape and only push play again when a "good" emotion showed up.

As you take inventory, keep in mind that these reactions and strategies *aren't bad*. We're all doing the best we can to be kind, genuine, wonderful human beings, and there is no need to beat yourself up for behaviors that spring out of good intentions for yourself or others. Rather, thank yourself for your good intentions, and keep on observing. Your inner doorbell camera is not a place for shame or self-recrimination. The whole point is to observe with neutrality, with the goal of gaining valuable information about yourself. The camera doesn't judge, and neither should you.

What Observing Isn't

Sometimes we think we're observing ourselves, when we're actually doing something quite different. Your brain can be sneaky, finding ingenious ways to keep you from doing the simple but courageous work of observation. This is especially true if it's in the habit of trying to protect you from thoughts and feelings it has deemed dangerous or bad.

Here are some things to remember if you find yourself sliding away from pure observation.

Observing isn't fixing! Most of us tend to skip observing and jump straight to fixing before we even know what the problem is—or even if there's a problem at all. We get so flustered by the *sensation* of the emotion—the sweaty palms, the tight chest—that we assume there must be a serious threat, and we react accordingly. This instinct to fix keeps us penned in our safe little boxes and robs us of the opportunity to grow. A friend of mine who struggles with social anxiety was always afraid that people would dislike her. Whenever this fear came up, she immediately tried to "solve the problem"—usually by fleeing the situation. But when she slowed down and observed her anxiety, she bought herself time to realize that her anxiety was a temporary feeling based on an exaggerated assessment of danger—just like the drunk guy who eventually stumbles away.

Observing isn't substituting! Substituting a "good" emotion for a "bad" one is really just a sneaky way to pass judgment. If you think that the thought or feeling you substitute is "good," it means you must have thought your original thought or feeling was "bad." For example, you assume that feeling grateful is better than feeling angry, or feeling cheerful is better than feeling depressed. But when you try to replace your true feelings with "better" ones, you inadvertently send yourself a message that you're too fragile to handle your emotions. This works against your own biology. Mental states like anger and sadness evolved for a reason. They're not bugs in the system; they're carefully designed *features*. They don't go away when you tell them to; they go away once you let them do their job. Suppressing so-called "negative" emotions cuts off a powerful thread of your own human experience—a thread you can come to value if you learn to use it appropriately. Try to be more like a doorbell camera—objective and free of judgment. When something "bad" surfaces, don't try to observe something "better." Just keep gazing straight ahead, taking in whatever you see.

Observing isn't goal-driven! It's easy to get stuck in the unconscious belief that the "point" of observing yourself is to change the things you don't like. One very frustrated client thought that, if she poured enough observation onto her thoughts and feelings, her emotional frogs would turn into princes—and she was disappointed and confused when this didn't happen. She assumed that her observational skills operated like a laser beam that could eventually "crack" her unwanted feelings once and for all. Without even realizing it, she had departed from a state of true observation—which is calm, receptive, and asks for nothing—and moved into a state of willful effort. She wanted so badly to see other emotions on her inner camera that she was generating frustration and distress—which were indeed new emotions, but not the ones she wanted.

The point of self-observation is not to get exactly the thoughts and feelings you want. On the contrary, it's to gain a sense of peace and equanimity with whatever thoughts and feelings do present themselves, whether they are princes or frogs. Self-observation should be a relatively peaceful state, not a strenuous effort or struggle. It entails *watching*, not *doing*. The moment you catch yourself *doing* is the moment you need to reset and start again.

It's Not All Shit

One amazing thing you discover as you get into observer mode is that it's not all shit. All those thoughts and feelings you've spent your whole life trying to ignore, or deny, or fix? They're not usually as scary as you think they are. When you let yourself feel a "difficult" emotion like sadness or disappointment, it tends to have a healing effect. Fear of the emotion is usually worse than the emotion itself—just like pulling a splinter out of your hand, or ripping a bandage off your ankle. And even more important, when you look away from your difficult emotions, you miss a whole lot of positive ones. It's like declining to go on a hike because you're afraid of bears. You certainly won't see any bears if you don't go on the hike, but you'll also miss out on the birds, the wildflowers, and the beautiful mountain landscapes.

I had a client who was terrified of her own sexuality. Any time a person flirted with her, she panicked. As she worked with self-observation over many months, she saw that pattern play out again and again. But as she observed her fear and unease, she noticed something incredible. Before these feelings appeared, she felt a tiny flicker of excitement and joy. The fear and unease weren't the first emotions she experienced; they were a substitution her brain was making to keep her safe. When she kept an eagle eye on her reactions, she detected this hidden joy before it slipped away. All her life, she'd been avoiding the bears, but the moment she went looking for them, she discovered the wildflowers as well.

Another client of mine had never let herself feel anger toward her parents for the harsh way they'd raised her and her siblings. Whenever that anger came up, she pushed it aside, telling herself that there was no point in getting angry after all these years. When she finally let herself feel her anger, she realized that it was swiftly followed by a heart-melting wave of compassion toward herself and her brother and sister. By avoiding her anger, she'd also missed out on this feeling of tender compassion. The more she allowed this anger to surface, the more she experienced this wonderful, healing energy. It wasn't possible to have one without the other.

The truth is that your inner doorbell camera isn't just for observing scary or uncomfortable things. You can observe plenty of wonderful things as well and develop your capacity for happiness and enjoyment in the process. There may be drunks passed out on your doorstep sometimes, but there are also kindly neighbors who come to the door, and friends who arrive with their arms full of presents. And if you're not watching, you'll miss them all.

Try This:

* Set a reminder to go off a couple of times a day. When it dings, observe your emotions for thirty seconds. How are you feeling? When did it start? How is it changing?

* The next time you feel an uncomfortable emotion, pretend you're on the other side of the door, perfectly safe, watching it through your doorbell camera. How do your reactions change when you feel safe, as opposed to threatened?

Chapter 3

Observing Your Emotions

When I was in my late teens, I decided to get my first tattoo. Now, I am not a needle person, or a pain person, or any kind of thrill seeker, but I really wanted this tattoo. So I somehow sweet-talked my mom into believing it was something she also wanted me to do.

The weird thing about getting a tattoo is that you sign yourself up for this somewhat painful and gruesome experience. Think about it. You place yourself in a room with a stranger who stabs a needle into your skin again and again. It hurts; sometimes you bleed. And, depending on the size of the tattoo, it can go on for a long fucking time. If this were being done to you against your will, it would be terrifying! But for the most part, you *choose* to get that tattoo, and that makes the difference. Sure, it may still be a little uncomfortable or maybe even a little scary, but the fact that you chose the experience makes it your own.

The same applies to painful or uncomfortable experiences like bikini waxes, jumping into a cold plunge pool, or ordering *el pique con fuerza* when you go out to eat. I don't think many people innately love having hot wax ripped off their private parts, or being dunked in freezing-cold water, or having their eyes water with every bite of food. But there's something magical about choosing to do these things. Instead of being unpleasant, they become exciting, thrilling, and empowering. Instead of traumatizing us, they fill us with a sense of pride. "Yeah, I jumped off that cliff into the waterfall!" "Yeah, I got that piercing!" "Yeah, I asked them out!"

Believe it or not, the same applies to emotions. Right now, you probably experience certain emotions with aversion. Anger? "No, I don't wanna; get away!" Sadness? "Don't come near me with that thing; are you crazy?" Uncertainty? "Get it off me right now!" You don't choose these experiences. Quite the opposite. You want to scramble up out of that chair as quickly as you can, and you don't want that needle going anywhere near your arms. Instead of choosing to feel these emotions, you try to fix them, to avoid them, to judge them, or to swap them for better ones. They make you feel frightened and overwhelmed. But what if I told you that you can transform that anxiety by turning toward it and saying: "Guess what? I choose to feel you."

A client of mine was a chronic fixer. Whenever her teenage son came to her with a problem, she felt a surge of anxiety. What if he didn't handle it properly? What if it screwed up his whole life? Instead of letting herself feel the anxiety, she jumped straight to fixing her son's problem, which had the convenient side effect of making her anxiety go away. The only problem was that, every time she jumped in to fix something, her son got the message that he wasn't capable of coming up with his own solutions, while my client got the message that she couldn't handle her own feelings of anxiety.

We decided that, the next time her son came to her with a problem and she felt that surge of anxiety and the accompanying urge to fix it, she would quietly say in her head: "I choose to feel this anxiety." Then she would let herself feel it for at least the space of one breath before deciding what to do. Sure enough, it wasn't long before her son found himself in a tricky situation with his girlfriend and asked her to tell him what to say. Even though she was feeling a powerful urge to write the text for him, she remembered our agreement. She took her deep breath and chose to feel the anxiety. The moment she did that, she realized that she could handle her feelings. She didn't need to make them go away by fixing her son's problem. "How about you take a stab at it," she told him. "And if you want to show me before you send it, I'm happy to take a look."

Her son went to his room for a couple of hours. My client waited nervously in the living room, trying to read a book but wondering what he was saying to his girlfriend, whether he was screwing it up, and whether she should intervene. Finally, he came downstairs. "We worked it out!" he announced. "I'm picking her up at eight."

The feeling of joy and pride in her heart was overwhelming. By choosing to sit with her own anxiety, she'd paved the way to growth and freedom, not only for herself, but for her son as well. The more you work with difficult emotions like anxiety, the more you start to cherish the burst of happiness that comes when you successfully ride them out without reacting. It's thrilling and a little addictive—like getting a tattoo (of which I now have thirty-two and counting).

The Power of Choice

The moment we choose to feel our emotions fully—whatever emotions show up—we create an opportunity for the experience to be potent, transformative, and highly meaningful, instead of scary, overwhelming, and traumatic. Fear and excitement have a lot in common, physiologically speaking. Both increase the heart rate, cause breathing to speed up, make palms sweat, and create a state of expectancy. As far as our bodies are concerned, there is no difference between fear and excitement; they manifest in the same way. It's only our minds that make a distinction—"I'm so fucking scared" versus "I'm so fucking excited." But when we choose to feel our emotions, our minds are more likely to tell our bodies we're feeling excitement, not fear, and anticipation rather than dread.

But don't worry, I'm not suggesting that you march into the nearest tattoo parlor and get a full sleeve. We're going to start small. The next time you observe a positive emotion coming up to your inner doorbell camera, pause and say to yourself: "I am choosing to feel this happiness." Or: "I am choosing to feel this hope." Then give yourself a couple moments to do exactly that. Feel the state of happiness in your body and mind. Let it expand and show itself. When you're ready to move on, simply let your awareness travel somewhere else. Practicing with positive emotions can help you develop an attitude of calm acceptance toward your feelings, which comes in handy when you're ready to move on to more difficult emotions.

Another way to improve your tolerance for difficult emotions is to practice with sensory experiences. Try putting your hand in a bowl of ice water for a few seconds. Really try to feel the sensation of cold—lean into it. Make it your own. Or try taking a bite of lemon, or diving into a yoga stretch you normally avoid, or engaging with some other benign-but-uncomfortable sensory experience. Realize that you can feel the discomfort without being in actual danger, and that your discomfort actually decreases when you make a conscious choice to feel those uncomfortable sensations. When you've gotten the hang of these two exercises, you can move on to choosing to feel more difficult emotions.

A friend of mine was grieving the impending loss of her home and community after making the difficult decision to move away to take care of her aging parents. The grief was so powerful that she was afraid that, if she let herself feel even a little bit of it, she would never stop crying. She tried to cheer herself up by thinking of things to look forward to in her parents' town, and by telling herself that her rambling old house was too much to take care of anyway. Bet you can guess how well that worked! Next, she tried to scold herself for being sad when she still had it better than most people. That didn't work either. The grief kept showing up again and again, even though she kept trying different ways to hold it off.

Finally, she had to accept that her strategies weren't working. She was going to have to feel the grief one way or another. The only question was whether it was going to be traumatic, or whether she could draw some healing from it. She chose one couch in her living room and designated it "the sad couch." She decided that, whenever she was sitting or lying on that couch, she would let herself cry, grieve, and feel her emotions fully.

At first, she only sat on "the sad couch" for five minutes at a time. The feelings were damned intense, and she didn't want to stay there for too long, especially because she still had to cope with the hard work of packing up her possessions and getting her house ready to sell. But these short sessions had the effect of building trust. She realized that the sad feelings felt good in a way and that, when she got off the couch, she could safely disengage and not be overwhelmed. Later, she started looking forward to her time on "the sad couch" because she realized that choosing to cry was helping her move through the grieving process.

When you feel afraid of a certain emotion, it's usually because you assume that that one feeling is the end of the road. If you give in to your grief, you fear that you will feel grief forever. If you dive into your anger, you fear you'll be stuck with it for the rest of your life. But the truth is that, when you hold off on feeling your emotions, that's when you get stuck with them. The best way to release an emotion is to process it fully, thereby moving it through the pipeline and allowing other emotions to appear in its wake. Personally, I've noticed that, when I let myself feel a difficult emotion, it's usually followed by two or three positive ones. By feeling the difficult ones, you allow the positive ones to come through.

Get Real with Your Emotions

In the last chapter, I talked about the importance of being honest with your observations. This is especially true when it comes to observing your emotions. We've been socialized since birth to show pleasing emotions for the benefit of others. And we may even have developed a lifelong habit of trying to fool ourselves. It can be tempting to lie about how we feel to preserve our self-image as nice, grateful, reasonable people. "Oh, I'm just so pleased my mother-in-law is going to move in with us! And she's bringing that adorable dog with her, the one that loves chewing furniture." We all want to look good to ourselves and others and, for many of us, that can easily turn into a kind of dishonesty.

But you can't fool yourself. Emotions are physiological. You can tell yourself that you're feeling calm and peaceful, but if your heart is beating rapidly, your body knows something exciting is happening, whether it's positive or negative. You can tell yourself that you're in love with someone, but if your pupils don't dilate when you're around that person and you experience an involuntary wave of disgust when you take a deep whiff of their scent, your body is clearly calling you out on the lie. If you're not in touch with your body, however, you can either miss or misinterpret these cues.

I once worked with a client who was unable to acknowledge her own anger. She absolutely denied that she ever felt angry about anything, and I knew that couldn't possibly be true. I asked her if she'd be willing to make a conscious attempt to get angry, right there in our session. There had recently been a police shooting in our city, so we started talking about that. As you can imagine, being a Black woman, I'd been rallying against racial injustice for years, so it was easy for me to generate topics that would get us both pretty riled up. With some encouragement from me, my client was able to connect with a real feeling of anger. Her voice sharpened, her posture straightened, and she felt a sense of heat in her body.

Once she had experienced that intentionally generated anger, she was able to recognize and acknowledge anger when it showed up in other places. As it turned out, this woman had a lot to be angry about, but she was so quick to distract herself from that feeling that she scarcely had time to notice when it was there. By inviting anger to show up, she built trust in herself that it was something she could feel, handle, and even appreciate as a natural and healthy response. Not only that, but she started to engage in activist work, unlocking a deep well of power that had been inaccessible as long as she was avoiding her anger.

Another client of mine was avoiding how unhappy she was in her relationship. When she was with her partner, she distracted herself by playing with her dog, telling herself that the happy feelings she experienced while doing it were representative of the relationship in general. She also enjoyed her job and loved her friends, and she thought that the happiness she experienced in these domains could somehow compensate for the sense of emptiness she felt in her relationship. It was only when she let herself admit how unhappy she was with her partner that she was able to grieve, take appropriate action, and move on to a truly happy life.

When you choose to feel your full range of emotions, you open up the possibility of making real changes in your life. When you avoid your emotions, you may experience a temporary feeling of relief. But in the long run, you're simply cutting off your own potential and hampering your ability to respond effectively to the true conditions of your life. Until this client could admit how unhappy she was, she could never take the courageous steps required to obtain true happiness. Until my other client could admit how angry she was, she could never step into her power as a social-justice activist.

If I find myself avoiding a certain emotion, I like to use one of the following phrases to build up my courage so I can choose to feel it:

* "I have handled this in the past. I am capable of this."

* "I'm stressed as shit, but I've been stressed like this many other times in my life and I've gotten through it. This is going to be another one of those times."

* "It's not time to worry yet."

* "I may not know how to solve this problem, but I can feel these feelings."

Reminding myself of my own competence, resilience, and creativity gives me the courage I need to lean into uncomfortable emotions and discover the great gifts that are waiting for me on the other side.

Know Your Patterns

A wonderful side benefit of observing your emotions is that you can use that self-knowledge to create more harmonious relationships with others. For example, one thing I've discovered through my own process of observation is that my sadness tends to come off as anger. Before I developed the habit of self-observation, it was easy for me to confuse my sadness with anger, and I could get into all sorts of conflicts as a result. My sadness often came across as confrontation: "Don't fucking talk to me; don't look at me; don't ask if I'm OK, I don't want to hear it. Leave me alone. Leave me the fuck alone!" Even my close friends sometimes thought I was angry with them. Hell, sometimes *I* wondered if I was angry at them! None of us understood that, when I lashed out or withdrew and stopped making eye contact, it was actually my sadness manifesting.

As you begin to practice self-observation, you will start to notice your own patterns. For example, you may find that, when you are dealing with overwhelming feelings, you retreat into solitude. This is not necessarily a bad thing. Maybe time with your thoughts gives you the space and perspective you need at that moment. On the other hand, you may be hiding and numbing your feelings in your aloneness. Recognizing these patterns can help you identify the actions you need to take to reach your larger goals, and it can also help you communicate more clearly with your friends, your family, and your partner.

When your brain takes in new experiences, it automatically begins to associate them with past experiences that are familiar. "The last time I felt scared, I left the party and drove away. That kept me safe last time, so I should probably do it again." When you're in observer mode, however, you can watch your brain go through this automatic process. The mere act of observing opens up the possibility for your brain to take new paths. "The last time I felt scared, I left the party and drove away. That kept me safe, but I also missed the party! Maybe this time, I'll try something different."

If you want to add an extra layer of intentionality to your observation practice, try asking yourself the following questions:

* What am I feeling?

* Why do I feel this way?

* Do I normally feel this way in this situation, or is this new?

* What's going on in my body?

* What do I want to feel?

* What's stopping me from feeling what I want to feel?

* Where else have I felt similar feelings?

* What do I need to have or do to begin feeling the way I want to feel?

These simple questions, when answered with honesty and intention, can help you examine your inner workings closely and see what makes you tick.

A friend of mine had been in a relationship with her boyfriend for three years. When she was alone, she thought of him fondly and loved texting him to say how much she missed him. But when she was with him, she often felt impatient and distracted. By observing herself closely, she realized that the part of their relationship she liked best was the anticipation of seeing him. She wanted to enjoy their time together, but that wasn't the same thing as actually enjoying it. She realized that she'd been staying in the relationship based on this false emotion and, when she got in touch with her real feelings, she decided to leave.

Another friend of mine felt worn down by her kids' hyperactive behavior at dinner time. Just when she most needed to relax after a hard day at work, they started bouncing off the walls. After observing her emotions in detail, however, she realized something that surprised her. *She* was the one who was wound up at mealtimes, not her kids. She came home exhausted and depleted, but her mind was still whirring with thoughts about unfinished projects. Her kids weren't any more energetic than usual; she was just reacting to them in an extreme way because she herself was feeling tense. She wanted to feel relaxed, but she wasn't quite there yet.

Uncovering what you want to feel reveals a lot about both where you are and where you want to be. Acknowledging that you want to feel something else—about your job, your relationship, your living situation, or anything—is a powerful first step in changing your life.

Stop Controlling; Start Observing

When you keep your observer mode switched on, you become an active participant in your own life. Emotions come to visit, but you have no reason to fear them. Because you have less fear, you feel less need to control your external reality. You can stay flexible and take things as they come; you can open yourself to new experiences and discover new strengths. You find that your internal self feels more free, more flowing, and more integrated. You stop wylin'—at least, when you don't want to. Because, let's be real, there's a time and a place for letting loose and wylin' out.

When you activate your observer mode, you learn that what you *can* control is enough. When I think back to that "bad dad text," I realize there were a million ways in which I could have responded better. I can't go back and change that. I can, however, develop the emotional skills to handle future crises more smoothly. My observer mode has helped me do exactly that. It helps me gain information about myself so I can use it to grow in the future. As unfortunate as that text was, I'm grateful for what came of it, because it catapulted me onto a path of self-observation, which has since helped me live a more peaceful life.

Learning about yourself is rarely easy. We're all flawed. But recognizing that you aren't *just* flawed can help you move forward. By observing your joy along with your sadness, your pride, creativity, and kindness along with your irritability, you can come to appreciate your full range of potential as a human being. I'm grateful for the side of me that has the capacity to wyle the fuck out when necessary, and for other parts of me that reflect the joy and calm in which I'm usually enveloped.

Try This:

* The next time your inner doorbell camera catches a difficult emotion walking up to the door, say out loud: "I choose to feel this anger/sadness/irritation/uncertainty." See what happens. Does your relationship to the emotion change?

* Come up with your own list of affirmations to say when you're getting ready to face a difficult emotion. For example: "I've been sad before and I've gotten through it. I can handle feeling sad now."

Chapter 4

Inner Voices and Familiar Faces

One of the cool features of my friend's doorbell camera is its ability to recognize familiar faces. After it's been watching for long enough, the camera starts to recognize people who show up on a regular basis, whether they be friends, delivery people, or unwanted lurkers. My friend can even go into the app and give these familiar people names, whether or not she knows them. Now she gets an alert on her phone when Hot UPS Guy is at her door, and she doesn't have to stumble over the burrito wrappers and Tecate cans to know that Obnoxious Lurker #1 and Obnoxious Lurker #2 were using her front doorstep as an after-hours club the night before.

I like to think of the voices in my head in the same way—as visitors who each have their own unique personality, quirks, and behaviors. My head is a busy place, much like my friend's street in San Francisco. From the moment I wake up in the morning, there's always one voice or another who is stuck to me like glue, chattering away throughout the day and even into the night in my dreams. My own inner dialog takes place 24/7. There's no escaping these voices, and they have something to say about everything—external events, internal experiences, and fantastical scenarios that haven't happened yet and may never happen.

For most of us, the voices in our heads constantly narrate what's happening, express concern about every single fear, and hype us up when we know we did something amazing. They share advice, direct and redirect us, and rehearse conversations before they happen (or suggest killer comebacks after the fact). At times, an inner voice may scream at you, berate you, point out your flaws, predict outcomes, or bemoan your fate. A different voice may offer loving reminders, encouragement, and empathy.

Our inner voices run on autopilot. They can be supportive, but they can also be mean, limiting, or intimidating. Some of us carry around veritable bullies in our heads, letting them speak to us in ways we would never stand for in real life. These voices have as much (or even more) influence on us as what's going on in the external world. That's why observing and becoming conscious of the quality and tone of your inner voices is so important.

Where Do Inner Voices Come From?

Our inner voices take shape during early life experiences. Some that show up in internal dialogs and monologs come from our parents or primary caregivers. A client of mine had an inner voice that was always reminding her not to be late. Whenever she was getting ready for work or even for a casual event like a party, the voice breathed down her neck, telling her to move a little bit faster. The voice clearly believed that being late was a terrible fate that must be avoided at all costs. It took my client months to realize that this voice belonged to her mother, who was extremely anxious about always being on time. She remembered the way her mother hovered by the door, checking her watch and fussing with her purse, clearly crawling out of her skin with desperation to get on the road so they wouldn't be late.

When my client examined herself closely, she realized that she did not, in fact, share this extreme phobia. She was just so used to living with this voice in her head that she had taken on her mother's anxiety as her own. As soon as she recognized this voice as her mother's and not her own, much of its power drained away. She even started talking back to it, saying: "It's okay, Mom, nobody is going to be mad if we're a few minutes late." Or: "Remember the last time we showed up for dinner at 6:00 PM and nobody else was there yet? It's *better* to show up a little late sometimes."

Another client had a kind voice in her head that was always looking out for her. "Remember your sweater," the voice would say. Or: "You left your keys in the pocket of your jeans, so don't panic because you're going to find them right there." No matter how flustered or overwhelmed she felt, this voice always knew exactly what to do. It radiated gentle kindness all the time, and she could always rely on it to take good care of her when she was feeling down. After exploring it in our session, my client realized that this kindly voice belonged to her grandmother, who had raised her and her brother from the time they were six and four years old until they were thirteen and fifteen. Even though her grandmother had died many years ago, she had left my client with the gift of this calm, practical, and protective voice to guide her through her days.

Cliché though it may be, children are sponges. They absorb everything thrown their way, and don't usually have the ability to analyze this input critically or make a conscious decision to accept or reject it. As children, we pick up on both the positive and negative attitudes our parents have, not only toward their children, but also toward themselves, their friends, their work, and other family members. When we're growing up, we hear our parents' or guardians' voices more frequently than any other voices. It's no wonder their most common refrains take up residence in our minds.

My friend's mom always used to talk to herself and other drivers on the road when we were in the car. We would listen as she snapped: "I'm so stupid. Why did I come this way? The traffic is terrible." Or: "Get the fuck off my ass! Jeez, what a jerk." As an adult, my friend often finds herself doing the same thing, constantly criticizing both herself and other drivers while on the road. She feels she inherited this voice from her mother, the same way she inherited her mother's books and clothes. Even though she hasn't yet managed to get rid of the voice, she has learned to laugh at herself every time she opens her mouth to gripe about another driver's skills.

Think about how your parents or caregivers spoke to you. Which of these messages, both positive and negative, are still playing in your head? Can you identify a distinct voice that belongs to one of your parents or caregivers? How much does this voice overlap with your true feelings, beliefs, and values? By looking back at your life history, you can arrive at a state of greater compassion for the negative voices in your mind, and gratitude for the helpful ones. You can feel less judgment toward yourself, knowing that, when you were a child, your brain was only doing what it was designed to do—absorbing anything and everything it could.

Familiar Faces

Do you have a voice in your head that comes to visit so often that it feels as if it practically lives with you—or worse, *is* you?

One client I worked with for over a year had been battling a nasty, critical inner voice for what felt like her entire life. This voice dictated her daily activities, sapped her energy, and dampened her moods. "Are you seriously going to wear that?" it would ask. Or: "You think those neighbors actually like you? Keep dreaming. They only invited you to be polite."

Even when my client was celebrating her biggest moments, like her wedding or the birth of her daughter, this nasty voice found a way to be heard. Whenever she felt joyous and at ease, she suddenly heard the voice saying: "Oh, you think this is going to last?" Although she knew in her heart that the voice came from a deeply wounded part of herself, and that she absolutely shouldn't take its admonitions too seriously, a sense of doubt still crept into her mind, blunting her joy and vitality.

This client had worked as a teacher for four years and was truly loved by her students and their families. After hearing that there was an opening for a specialty subject teacher in the same school, she put herself up for the position and got the job, not only because she was qualified, but because she stood out among the other candidates. But her knowledge that others had applied for the job left her feeling insecure. That critical voice started whispering in her ear, and she began to wonder if she really *was* the best candidate for the position.

Soon, her critical voice became relentless. It talked to her from the moment she woke up in the morning until the moment she went to bed at night. Its attacks were particularly harsh when she was around her colleagues, changing the way she related to them. The voice in her head prompted her to ask herself: "Are they wondering if I'm good enough?" This uncertainty made her cagey and insecure, which in turn made colleagues feel uncomfortable around her.

To break the cycle, we decided to personify this inner voice to give her some distance from it. She gave it the name Mrs. Brittleblocker to make herself laugh and remind her that the voice was not, in fact, *her*, but a character she had created from a collection of negative moments or people in her life. When the voice showed up in her head, she imagined this irritating character ringing her doorbell, wanting to be let inside. She realized that, even though she could hear Mrs. Brittleblocker chattering away, she was under no obligation to let her inside the house. The more clearly she established this boundary, the more she created space for other, more helpful voices to be heard.

Just as a doorbell camera can generate a list of familiar people who come to the door, you can generate your own list of "familiar faces" for the voices in your head, and give yourself some distance from them in the process. By using your skills of honest, non-judgmental observation, you can identify your most prominent voices and develop a healthier relationship with them.

My work with my own inner voices began with simply observing and then accepting what was happening inside my head. Sometimes I wrote it out in my journal; sometimes I spoke into a voice memo; sometimes I focused on inner listening. Within a short time, I had to acknowledge that most of my inner dialog wasn't kind. I was talking down to myself when I made mistakes, constantly second-guessing my abilities and criticizing myself for all the ways I could be better and do more at every point of my day, even when it came to things I didn't care about! My most prominent inner voice was forever shaming me for all that I wasn't doing. Who was this person? Why was I allowing her to reign supreme in my head? Something needed to change—drastically.

I gave this voice the name Yappy Dog, because it reminded me of a small, high-strung creature always snapping at my heels, chasing me from one task to the next. Thinking of this voice as an annoying, yappy dog drained a lot of its power. After all, am I seriously going to take orders from a shih tzu? After observing it for a long time, I realized that this voice had good intentions, even if it was going about things in the wrong way.

Yappy Dog wanted to help me achieve my goals, and the only way it knew how to do that was to bark at me. This realization helped me feel more compassion toward this voice, and less irritation.

Eventually, I even came to feel *fond* of Yappy Dog. It had become so harmless to me that I could see past its constant yapping to the real affection and protectiveness that lay beneath. I wanted to make sure that, while I was becoming fond of Yap, I was also leaving room for the growth I wanted to see and feel within. I continued to focus on and praise its good intentions and tried to redirect the actions of unsolicited advice and criticism. Before I knew it, Yappy Dog ceased to be a source of distress and became something more like a quirky sidekick.

Tame Your Voices

When you observe an inner voice, first take note of how often it comes up. Look for patterns. Does it show up when you're hungry? In the morning more than at night? In social situations or when you're alone? When you're sore and in pain after tweaking your back? Paying attention to these patterns will help you understand what the voice is trying to achieve. Once you understand that, you can feel more compassion toward it and help it achieve its goals in a way that doesn't shrink your life, harm your self-esteem, or otherwise drive you crazy.

For example, a friend of mine had an inner voice that always piped up when she was nervous about an upcoming social interaction. It rehearsed different things she could say, came up with funny stories she could tell, and practiced vulnerable confessions she could share. She often found herself spending hours listening to this voice, when the actual social interaction lasted only five minutes. Not only that, but her rehearsing left her feeling *more* rigid and stilted in social situations. The clever things she planned to say fell flat, because they didn't come at the right time or the conversation didn't take the direction she expected.

It was clear to her that this mental rehearsing was a big waste of her time and energy. Yet once this inner voice started filling her head with helpful suggestions, she couldn't find a way to turn it off. She named this voice the Stage Director, because it was endlessly drilling her on her lines, and even giving her advice on where to sit and stand, or how to move her body.

I encouraged her to look for the voice's intention. What was it trying to achieve? What was it trying to prevent? Even if they're nasty, irritating, or glum, our inner voices usually have good intentions for us, and identifying those good intentions can be the first step in building a better relationship with them. After all, our brains are survival machines. Their only job is to help us stay safe and avoid dying. With few exceptions, our brains are *always* trying to help us survive. That nasty voice in your head telling you that you look terrible may actually derive from a good intention that you can uncover if you dig deep enough. Maybe it's trying to protect you from the shame and embarrassment of leaving the house with spinach between your teeth. No matter how exhausting, irritating, mean, or contemptuous they are, our voices always have the goal of protecting us and ensuring our survival, even if they're going about it in a ridiculous way.

After listening and observing for a while, my client realized the Stage Director was truly trying to be helpful. She had suffered from severe social anxiety as a child, and it often felt safer to imagine social interactions than to experience them in real life. She had had a few painful incidents in her teens, in which she had gone to a social event and talked to no one because she was too shy. She suspected that the Stage Director had evolved out of her desire to make sure that this embarrassing situation never happened again. As an adult, she had learned to enjoy interacting with other people, but the Stage Director was still concerned that she would run out of things to say and humiliate herself. To protect her from this horrible fate, this voice tried to make sure she always had plenty of material prepared in advance.

Once she realized that this voice was doing its best to help her, my client felt far less distress when it made itself heard. She even started talking back to it: "Oh

Stage Director, I know you're trying to help me come up with interesting things to say, and I appreciate your good intentions. But I want you to know that I feel totally confident about this social interaction, and I'd like to chatter away without planning what I'm going to say in advance."

When she started talking to this voice with kindness and appreciation, it slowly began to cooperate. It was as if it understood that it wasn't needed anymore, and was content to wait in the wings until she chose to call on it for help. Whatever threat to her survival the Stage Director had perceived in the past had seemingly lessened. In the process of easing this voice out of her head, my client was also affirming to herself that she was doing alright and wasn't in need of direction. Following through with her statements to the Stage Director proved to her that she *was* capable, not just of getting through an unscripted social interaction, but of fully enjoying it.

If you are working with a difficult or intrusive inner voice, I encourage you to try a similar strategy. Ask yourself what your voice is trying to achieve and how it's trying to protect you. Our inner voices are often trying to protect us from shame, humiliation, and failure. If we can reassure them that those threats are not as bad as they imagine, they sometimes feel comfortable stepping down. Remind your inner voice of all the times you have successfully handled the feared situation, and gently ask it to give you a chance to face new situations without its help.

Quiet the Nag; Welcome the Friend

A client once said to me: "We're the first voice we hear in the morning, so why not have us hear a kind and loving voice the second we open our eyes?"

Think of the excitement with which a pet greets you in the morning, or how loving parents say hello to their children as they wake up. You can cultivate the same quality of tender care toward yourself by speaking to yourself in a warm and loving way, even if the events in your life aren't going exactly as you planned. You can respond to setbacks with a sense of humor, and practice keeping a broad perspective instead of tunneling in on a small set of details.

One of the voices in my head used to nag me mercilessly whenever I saw others my age doing well in their careers or reaching milestones I longed to attain myself. "It's because they're better at their jobs than you are at yours," it would say. Or: "You're not working hard enough. You're not engaging enough. Maybe you *aren't* enough." If these words had come out of the mouth of a friend or family member, I would've shut that person down in a heartbeat. Yet many of us accept harsh, critical words from ourselves that we would never accept from others.

To counter this critical voice—which I dubbed the Nag—I decided to invite in a new voice I called the Friend. The Friend always spoke in a voice of wisdom, compassion, and gentle humor. "Maybe their journey isn't comparable to yours," she would say, when I felt I was falling behind my peers. Or: "Maybe you're working hard enough for your path." Or: "You're engaging in these ways and you're enough in these areas."

The Friend came from my higher self, and she expressed my highest values. When the Nag told me I wasn't achieving enough, she reminded me that life is about more than racking up achievements. When the Nag tried to make me speed up, she reassured me that I was already going as fast as I needed to go. I came to understand that, while the Nag came from a place of fear, anxiety, and control, the Friend was tapped into a sense of expansiveness, trust, and equanimity. You may call this voice your authentic self, your inner angel, or anything else that feels meaningful to you.

The more you cultivate this Friend, the less powerful your own personal Nag becomes. You can trust in life and stop trying to control everything, knowing that your Friend will always be there for you. Instead of struggling against darkness and negativity, you can simply allow it to drop away. And you can greet your familiar faces without fear.

Try This:

* Try talking back to your "familiar faces." Acknowledge their good intentions, then tell them what you want. For example, say: "Hey Nag, I know you're trying to protect me from humiliation. You must care about me to put this much thought into how I look and act. I know you only want the best for me. But I'd like to try to do this task without your help."

* Experiment with developing your own version of the Friend. Your Friend may be soothing: "Oh my love, I know things feel so hard right now. I see you're in pain. Everybody feels disappointed/sad/lonely sometimes." It may be encouraging: "I can do this, I got this. I'm resourceful and strong. I love a good challenge." It may be truth-telling: "I'm going to tell myself the whole truth, even if it scares me. No more hiding to make myself safe. Secrets hurt more." Or it may be reflective: "Look at how far you've come! You're so different and handle things more calmly than you used to."

Chapter 5

Safety Dances and Daring Dances

When I was in my early twenties and living in New York City, I met a charming guy. He was handsome and attentive, and noticed every little thing about me. Before long, we were head over heels in love—and that's when the problems began. What started out as attentiveness turned into intense jealousy. He wanted to know where I went, whom I saw, and what I did with every minute of my day. If I didn't dress the way he thought was cool, he pointed out the so-called problems with how I looked. If I spent time with my friends, he accused me of neglecting him. If I so much as made eye contact with another guy, he accused me of being sus.

Thanks to the help of my friends and family, I managed to leave this abusive relationship after only three months. But, even though the relationship was short, it affected me in profound and lasting ways. Months after I had left, I still found myself avoiding eye contact with strangers. I was reluctant to leave the house unless I looked perfect, and I rehearsed everything I said before I said it just to make sure I said the "right" thing. I made some practical changes to keep myself safe from my ex-boyfriend—like riding a different subway route to work—but the behaviors I had difficulty shaking had nothing to do with this kind of basic safety. Rather, they were inhibiting my contact with others—including perfectly nice people!—unless I felt I had complete control over the situation.

Looking back, I can see that I was experiencing a high degree of anxiety, and that these behaviors were simply my attempt to manage that anxiety. I believed I would only be "safe" if I could eliminate all uncertainty. With that in mind, I put 100 percent of my energy into avoiding situations and social interactions in which I wasn't completely sure what would happen. Shit, I wouldn't even open a gift in front of someone whose reaction I couldn't accurately predict. I didn't trust others, and I certainly didn't trust myself. I felt I always had to think ahead in order to predict what would happen and preempt the many bad scenarios my brain concocted.

I now think of those behaviors as my "safety dance"— an elaborate and exhausting set of moves I continually ran through to protect myself from both real and imaginary dangers. Like a physical dance, this mental two-step burned a lot of energy and sometimes required a lot of concentration. At the time, however, I didn't realize I was trapped in this dance. I truly believed that, if I stopped trying to eliminate uncertainty, I would be overwhelmed by frightening, humiliating, and anxiety-provoking experiences. I believed I was *that fucking good*—that my avoidance and rigid attempts at control were what was keeping my life from spinning into absolute chaos.

What Is a Safety Dance?

A safety dance is all about control. It's a set of behaviors that temporarily reduce anxiety and protect you from whatever you fear most—whether that's being the object of another person's anger or irritation, being humiliated, or simply being caught unprepared. The problem with safety dances is that they use a *ton* of energy, and they never end. You can't just check your appearance once and then feel confident forever; you have to check it again and again. You can't avoid eye contact once; you end up having to avoid it all the time. You can't seek a quick burst of reassurance just this once; you have to seek it over and over, from anyone who will give it.

It's easy to convince yourself that a safety dance will be required "just this once." You tell yourself that you have to avoid a particular person or refrain from engaging in a certain activity "just this once" because you feel too anxious today. So you hurry into the house when you see a difficult neighbor approaching because you don't have the energy to deal with the conflict. Or you keep quiet in a meeting, even though you have something important to say. And guess what? It works! Your safety dance really does help you avoid that difficult neighbor or the potential awkwardness of sharing your ideas in public. And this success appears to prove that the dance is actually effective. But before you know it, you find yourself avoiding and refraining 24/7, and it seems as if there's *never* a time when you're not too anxious to re-engage.

This is what makes safety dances so tricky, and so addictive—they work! When you avoid someone or decline to participate in an activity, you really do escape the anxiety that threatens to overwhelm you in the moment. But in the long run, this strategy traps you into even *more* anxiety, because, instead of confronting your fears and overcoming them, you fall back on avoidance all the time. Your life starts to shrink, becoming smaller and smaller until it occupies only the tiny footprint that your anxieties have carved out for you. When you eliminate uncertainty, you eliminate a wide range of other experiences—not only the negative ones you intended to get rid of, but positive ones as well. It's like using a pesticide to kill ants, but also wiping out the butterflies, bees, and other beneficial insects without which a garden can't thrive. When you put your anxieties in charge, the first thing they do is cannibalize your joys. This is why it's so important to recognize when you're engaged in a safety dance, and take the necessary action to break the cycle.

Safety Dances in Action

A client of mine struggled with making decisions. When she thought of something she wanted to do—in her case, start a dog-grooming business—she went around to everyone she knew and asked them whether they thought she should carry out her plan. The moment someone encouraged her to open her business, she told them all the reasons she shouldn't do it. And whenever a friend or family member expressed reservations about her plan, she got upset with them for not supporting her dreams. Instead of making a decision, she just kept drawing out the decision-making process by seeking more and more opinions. Yet no matter how many opinions she got, she still never made up her mind.

Although she couldn't admit it to herself, my client was engaged in an elaborate safety dance whose goal was to ensure that she never made a "bad" decision. By remaining in the "research" phase, keeping her options open, and seeking endless opinions, she never had to face her fear of committing to a specific course of action. She wore out her friends and acquaintances by engaging them in never-ending conversations about her dilemma, and frequently felt depressed and anxious because her life wasn't going anywhere. Her safety dance was indeed protecting her from what she feared, but in the process, it was taxing her relationships and eating away at her self-esteem.

In our session together, we decided to set a time limit. She gave herself twenty-four hours to decide once and for all whether to start her dog-grooming business, after which she would forever hold her peace. Not only that, but, within that twenty-four hours, she was prohibited from seeking any more advice from her already maxed-out friends and family. Those twenty-four hours were sheer torture for her. The urge to call just one friend or family member for yet another round of advice was overwhelming. But she made it through and, the next time we met, she told me that she had decided to move forward. Over the next few months, she experienced many moments of anxiety when things didn't go as planned. But one year later, she had a successful business up and running, and she was grateful that she hadn't wasted any more time sitting on the fence.

Another client didn't feel comfortable going to social events unless she had thoroughly grilled the hosts—and not just in the "Who's going to be there?" kind of way. Her list of essential questions was extensive, to say the least. What time would the event start? How long would it last? How loud would the music be? What would the temperature be like—should she bring a sweater or a bathing suit? Would there be food, or should she eat first, or bring her own snacks? What was the parking situation like? Should she arrive early to get a spot? She felt that, if she could gather enough information about the event, she would somehow be better equipped to handle it. Yet no matter how much information she gathered, she could always think of more questions to worry over.

This client's safety dance was geared toward eliminating uncertainty—all uncertainty. She always tried to peer into the future, living out events before they happened. Although her dance helped her to prepare for a wide variety of situations, it drained her of spontaneity and shrank her life to include only those events for which she felt prepared and that she knew would go well. This kept her in a state of unnecessary anxiety about her own ability to tolerate the unpredictable. Because she always planned everything carefully, she never had the opportunity to find out that she could, indeed, adapt to situations for which she was unprepared.

We decided that, the next time she was invited to a party or other social event, she would not seek any more information than what was included in the invitation. In fact, she wouldn't even let herself read the invitation in detail until half an hour before the event was supposed to start. This lack of preparation was very, very uncomfortable for her. She was certain she would arrive late, or wear the wrong clothes, or run into people she didn't want to see, or go hungry if she guessed wrong about the food being served. But when it came down to it, she had a great time. She hadn't realized how much her preparations were winding her up and surrounding her with a cloud of anxiety that was detectable to others. In fact, people liked her better when she showed up a little flustered than when she showed up a half hour early, completely prepared but no fun.

I spent most of my twenties believing that others would only like me if I somehow looked and acted "perfect." I spent hours getting ready before I left the house, checking my reflection from every angle, and trying on two or three different outfits before deciding what to wear. In conversations with strangers, I was unfailingly polite, ingratiating, and solicitous. I rarely expressed my own feelings or opinions, and focused instead on making others feel good at any cost. Again and again, I found myself creating a whole new personality to please each person I talked to.

This safety dance ensured that I was well-liked by everyone—even those I did not actually like! In fact, it was almost too effective. Everybody thought I was their best friend because I was just that good at, well, making people feel good. For a long time, I thought this was an empath superpower. And it is! But it was a superpower I hadn't yet learned to wield appropriately. I believed that I *needed* to make other people feel good— had to keep their "happiness planets" spinning—even if this left me sitting silently in a corner. And no one puts baby in the corner.

Once I began to recognize my safety dance for what it was, I determined to change it. Although it was scary, I experimented with stating my true opinion, even when it conflicted with the opinion of the person with whom I was speaking. I backed off my excessive fawning and learned to save my smiles for when I was truly pleased by something. Although I feared people would start to dislike me, I was amazed when the opposite happened. My existing friendships grew closer and more authentic, and I made some new friends as well. When I was overly ingratiating, nobody could trust that I was sincere. When I began to step away from my safety dance and express my true self, people responded by sharing their true selves with me.

Identify Your Safety Dance

Identifying your safety dances can be difficult, because they often masquerade as reasonable, normal, "good" behaviors. It's normal and reasonable to seek opinions from your friends, research events you're planning to attend, and do your best to put others at ease. So how can you tell when something you're doing is part of a safety dance? Here are some questions to ask yourself:

What is the goal of this behavior? The whole point of a safety dance is to protect you from something you fear, even if it means giving up things you might otherwise value or enjoy. Ask yourself if your behavior has the goal of protecting you. Do you seek reassurance from friends because you are truly curious about their opinions, or because you want to delay making your own decision? Do you avoid coworkers because you don't like them, or because you're afraid you'll be awkward and say the wrong thing? If the motivation for your behavior is avoidance, that's a big clue you may be engaged in a safety dance.

Do I learn and grow from this behavior? Safety dances are about preserving the status quo. They give you a temporary feeling of security, but don't push you to grow. For example, a safety dance may involve showing up early for events so you don't have to face the anxiety of finding a seat in a crowded room. While this may prevent you from having to face an anxiety-provoking situation, it won't help you outgrow the anxiety itself. Safety dances keep you stuck in a limited space where you are defined by your fears and anxieties; they do not push you to face your fears and learn new skills.

What emotions do I feel when I engage in this behavior? Safety dances may provide a temporary sense of relief, but they are invariably followed by a fresh surge of anxiety that must then be quelled by yet another repetition of the behavior. They never bring lasting peace, because they do not address the root of your anxiety. They just help you side-step uncomfortable feelings for a short time. They may also cause you to experience feelings of dis-appointment or even shame, because, on some level, you know exactly what you're doing and are aware that your actions are limiting your life.

If these questions don't help you identify the moves in your own personal safety dances, see if any of these common dance moves apply to you:

* Seeking reassurance

* Demanding certainty

* Over-researching or over-planning

* Insisting on being prepared

* Avoiding anxiety-provoking situations

* Perfectionism

* Sticking to what you know

* Doing things the same way every time

* Refusing to do things alone or without help

* Refusing to attempt things you don't already know how to do

* Sticking to predictable scripts in social interactions

* Playing with your phone when you feel anxious

* Only going out and engaging in activities with a "safe" friend or relative

Remember, these behaviors are not "bad" in and of themselves. We all need reassurance sometimes, and we all have moments when we want a trusted friend by our side. But these behaviors turn into a safety dance when you rely on them repeatedly, with the goal of avoiding a situation that would probably help you grow if you could muster the courage to confront it.

Find Your Daring Dance

So what's the alternative to a safety dance? How about a daring dance? A daring dance is a set of moves that gives you the opportunity to feel your uncomfortable emotions, face your fears, and develop trust in yourself and in life. Whereas the goal of a safety dance is to protect you from anxiety-provoking situations at all costs, the goal of a daring dance is to expand your tolerance for these situations—in other words, to get comfortable with being uncomfortable. While a safety dance merely stops a real or imaginary bad thing from happening, a daring dance offers you the chance to get what you really want. In the words of Rainer Maria Rilke: "Our deepest fears are like dragons guarding our deepest treasure." When you engage in a daring dance, you walk right up to those dragons and increase the likelihood that you will find your own personal treasures.

A client of mine used to eat her lunch alone because it felt safer than sitting at a table with her college classmates and running the risk of having nothing to say. But this safety dance came at a high cost. Avoiding people wasn't exactly a great strategy for making friends. To transform her safety dance into a daring dance, she first identified what she wanted (friends and a social life!) and decided she could tolerate some discomfort to get them. The first time she sat down at a table with some girls from her dorm, she couldn't think of anything to say. It really was awkward, but it wasn't the devastating humiliation she'd imagined. The next time she joined them, she found a way to contribute to the conversation. Soon, she felt comfortable sitting with them whenever she felt like it, and her old anxiety was gone.

Another client was terrified of being seen as needy. She avoided asking for help with anything, even when it was more than reasonable to do so. She found clever ways to do difficult tasks alone, even when it took twice or even three times as long. Once, she even threw out her back moving a heavy couch by herself, because she was too afraid to ask a neighbor for help.

We decided she would start her daring dance by asking a close friend for a small favor—a ride to the airport. The thought of causing any inconvenience made her anxious and she worried that her friend might feel burdened by the request, but she summoned the courage and asked anyway. Although she felt anxious during the phone call, she tolerated the feeling and, when her friend showed up the next morning to pick her up, she felt a burst of happiness and pride. This was so much better than sticking to her safety dance and suffering through an hour-long bus ride. Her friend was perfectly happy to give her a ride, and they had a great time together, listening to music, drinking coffee, and catching up.

My client didn't *want* to spend her whole life taking the bus to the airport and moving heavy couches by herself. This was simply a pattern she'd fallen into to deal with her anxiety. When she took the leap of asking for help, she started to grow out of this old pattern and enjoy the kind of life she *did* want, filled with the normal exchange of favors that characterize healthy friendships and relationships. She realized that she could trust her friends—and people in general—to communicate their boundaries, instead of assuming they would allow themselves to be burdened in an unacceptable way.

As you work to develop your own daring dance, ask yourself these questions about the behaviors involved:

Do they help you move past old insecurities? Safety dances keep you stuck in one place. Daring dances are all about forward motion. Learning to tolerate and even embrace your uncomfortable feelings offers you amazing opportunities to break through old patterns and create the life you want. Daring dances teach you that you can stare down even your oldest, meanest dragons and find the treasure waiting on the other side— whether that's better friendships, a more fulfilling career, or anything else you can imagine.

Do they build your trust in yourself, other people, and life? Safety dances are based on the premise that you can't trust anyone or anything; all you can do is try to control reality as tightly as possible. But daring dances are all about trust. When you engage in a daring dance, you trust yourself to handle uncomfortable feelings. You trust that these feelings won't hurt you and that they will pass. And you trust that tolerating them is worth it for the rewards that await you on the other side. At the same time, you also build trust in the fact that you can be imperfect, awkward, weird, or unprepared, and others will generally continue to treat you in a kind and respectful manner.

Do they move you closer to your highest self? Safety dances keep you locked in a fearful, shrunken, rigid version of yourself— your lower self. They can cause you to give up so many things that make life worth living in exchange for a false and temporary sense of safety. But daring dances push you to reach for what you want, whether that's a better social life, a more interesting job, greater confidence in your appearance, or anything else. When you engage in a daring dance, you make a strong statement about what you value and who you want to be. You carve out a new identity for yourself that is more tightly matched to your highest aspirations. The price of this ambition is discomfort. But here's the good news. You soon learn that tolerating more discomfort is not such a high price to pay after all.

Do they restore your ability to be flexible, spontaneous, and free? Safety dances are about rigidity, control, and preparation. But daring dances are about gaining confidence in your own abilities, so they naturally cut down on your need for rigid control in your life. Think of the confident way you move through your own kitchen. You know where the pots and pans are; you know how to turn on the stove. With enough practice, a daring dance can give you that same level of confidence moving through *your entire life.* As you learn to trust that you can handle anything, you don't need to spend as much time and energy preparing for everything.

The more you engage in a daring dance, the more you expand your tolerance for discomfort. And the more you tolerate that discomfort, the more you receive the gifts of daring—flexibility, open-heartedness, spontaneity, and courage.

So instead of leaving these gifts gathering dust and out of reach, move those dragons out of the way and pull those treasures out of the cave and into the sunlight where they belong. You'll soon realize that you are strong enough to handle uncertainty, and resilient enough to adapt to situations for which you are not prepared. Best of all, your own state of freedom and self-acceptance creates a space where others feel empowered to be their true selves, thereby creating a positive cycle that benefits everyone around you.

Try This:

* Identify the moves you make in your own safety dances and write them down. The next time you notice yourself busting out one of these dance moves, notice how it makes you feel. Do you feel a deep and lasting sense of relief, or just a fleeting reduction in anxiety?

* Plan to replace at least one of your safety dances with a daring dance. What is one small change you can make to face your anxiety and develop confidence in yourself?

Chapter 6

Big Ups to Boundaries

Picture this: You're at the beach with your family. You have blankets and chairs and a beach umbrella. You brought food and cold drinks. You've got everything set up and are just about to break out the sandwiches when another group wanders across the huge, empty beach and starts setting up their blankets and chairs right next to yours—maybe even overlapping a little. Their big dog starts digging and kicking up sand all over your stuff. They reach over and help themselves to some chips, grab your sunscreen, and start tossing around the beach ball you brought for your kids. You feel as if you should say something, but you don't want to be rude, so you sit there awkwardly, waiting for them to go away.

Alternatively, imagine going to the beach and setting up your stuff, then rolling out caution tape in a thirty-foot radius around your spot. Whenever anyone gets near the tape, you pull out your trusty bullhorn and blast a verbal warning their way. You never end up swimming or having any beachy type of fun, because you're too busy patrolling the line, guarding your territory against interlopers.

If only it were always this easy to recognize whether your boundaries are way too weak or way too firm!

Thinking about boundaries can bring a twinge of discomfort. Almost all of us have had the awkward experience of setting a boundary with others, only to have them feel hurt, get mad, or complain. We've all had the experience of feeling guilty for setting a boundary, waiting too long to set a boundary, or letting someone's hurt or outrage control where the boundary gets set. But if you let these uncomfortable experiences stop you from setting boundaries, you end up staying in unhealthy situations and dealing with toxic people way longer than you should.

Without the ability to set boundaries, all you can do is *hope* that other people will stay an appropriate distance from your beach towels and keep their filthy paws out of your chip bowl. And even though this strategy can work for a while, it ultimately leaves you mired in anxiety, because you have no ability to assert yourself when others don't act the way you want them to.

Going through life without boundaries is like driving a car with no brakes, *hoping* you don't have to stop, and leaving yourself completely at the mercy of random forces—a strategy that doesn't exactly inspire confidence. In fact, you probably spend the whole time nervously scanning the road, imagining various worst-case scenarios, and desperately running through mental rehearsals of what you'll do if you see a pedestrian crossing the street ahead of you. But when your car has brakes, you don't need to be in constant fear when you drive, because you know that, if a situation arises that requires you to stop, you can do so.

A woman I know had no brakes whatsoever on her proverbial car. She owned a piece of land in a hippie town in California, and had a hard time saying no when friends, travelers, friends of friends, and even total strangers asked her for a place to stay. Over the years, her house had turned into an unofficial hostel, with people showing up unannounced, setting up camp under her oak trees or in her spare room, letting their dogs run loose, and coming and going as they pleased. Many of these people were very nice, and my friend enjoyed spending an evening or two in their company. But as word spread that her land was a free place to crash, a rougher sort of visitor began to appear—heavy drug and alcohol users who were hitchhiking through or hopping trains.

My friend didn't want to be accused of discriminating against anyone, so she let these questionable types camp on her land, even though she herself was not a substance user and felt uncomfortable with that energy. She was afraid of looking judgmental, cold-hearted, and a whole host of other negative things. As a practicing Buddhist, she feared it would be hypocritical of her to offer her generosity to some travelers but not others. Then one night, a group of heavy-drinking travelers started a campfire—a huge no-no in the dry season. As she stood looking out her kitchen window and watching the fire burn, she realized that her unwillingness to set boundaries had resulted in a truly dangerous situation, not just for herself, but for her entire community.

She called a neighbor and asked him to come over for backup. Then she walked over to the campfire with her garden hose, informed the campers that fires were not allowed, and instructed them to leave first thing in the morning. As she sprayed down the fire with water, she realized how close she had come to losing everything just because she was afraid that total strangers would think she wasn't "nice." Her desire to be seen as an infinitely generous, kind, long-suffering Buddha had severely impacted her ability to set appropriate boundaries until it was almost too late.

So how can you build your boundary-setting skills? The first step is merely to notice when something feels wrong to you. What feels like too much? What feels off? What feels like not enough? One clear sign that your boundaries are being violated is when you notice a feeling of tension building inside yourself. Another sign is when you repeatedly find yourself wanting to say something but holding back out of politeness, self-doubt, or fear of conflict. In my friend's case, she felt a definite pinch of tension when she saw the heavy-drinking visitors coming down the road, and more tension when they set up camp and built their fire. She wanted to intervene, but hesitated because she didn't want to come off as rude or controlling. In retrospect, she could tell these were signs that her boundaries were being violated—her body's way of informing her that something was wrong.

The next step is to fully embrace the awkwardness of drawing a line. We often refrain from setting boundaries because we don't want to face this awkwardness. It's like putting off going to the dentist. You know it's good to get your teeth cleaned, but you still avoid it until it's almost too late. But when you commit to the discomfort up front, knowing it will benefit you in the long run, it's easier to follow through with the appointment. Try telling yourself the boundary setting is only a temporary discomfort, whereas the lack thereof may bring longer-term discomfort. Give yourself a little nudge forward by affirming your choice with a simple statement like: "Damn, this is going to be awkward, but I'm choosing to do it anyway." This will put you in a bold, empowered mindset for setting your boundary.

Embrace Awkwardness

A friend of mine lives in a nice condo near the beach. She's a very sociable person, and one of the reasons she decided to live in a condo is that she loved the idea of being surrounded by friends and neighbors. People in the building love her, and are always stopping by to hang out, drop off treats and baked goods, or invite her to go swimming. One day, a new neighbor moved onto her floor, an eighty-year-old man who lived alone. Being the kind, warm-hearted person she is, my friend knocked on his door, introduced herself, and welcomed him to the building. He told her that he was a retired university professor in a field that interested her. She invited him to stop by for coffee someday to tell her about his research.

Before she knew it, he was coming to her door every day, sometimes multiple times a day. He didn't wait to be invited in, or ask if it was a good time. He just walked right in and sat down. As if that weren't bad enough, he didn't have anything interesting to say about his research. Instead, he spent hours complaining about his ingrown toenail. My friend felt badly for him, but she dreaded his visits. She didn't understand why he felt entitled to take up so much of her time. Where had she gone wrong? She was just trying to be kind. But now she was stuck with this guy, and she wanted her time back.

Because she felt too awkward to state a boundary, she did what most of us do instead. She started shrinking her life to avoid him. She kept her door closed instead of leaving it open to enjoy the ocean breeze. Whenever she heard a knock on her door, she felt an urge to duck because of the surge of anxiety that rushed through her body as she wondered if he were back. Because they saw her door closed and assumed she wasn't home, the neighbors she *did* want to see stopped coming over. Instead of asking the old man to change his behavior, she changed her own behavior in an attempt to compensate for his intrusiveness. In other words, she quietly paid the tab, while he continued to rack up the bills.

How many times have you shrunk your own life to avoid the awkwardness of telling someone what you need and want? Sure, it may seem easier to make a small adjustment rather than confronting others about their behavior. But before you know it, you start giving up things that are important to you and inviting unnecessary stress and anxiety into your life. You begin to get pulled into lower versions of yourself, perhaps becoming angry and resentful, or blaming others for behaviors they may not even realize are over the line.

I asked my friend what she would say to the old man if she could take a magic pill that could stop her from feeling any awkwardness whatsoever. She made a growling sound. "I would tell him to take a fucking hint and stop knocking on my damned door all the time!" she replied. "I work from home, and I'm not here to fucking entertain him all day. But he seems to think I'm permanently available."

I took a box of breath mints from my purse and gave her one. "Here's your magic pill," I said. "Now walk down the hall, knock on his door, and set that boundary—maybe a little more gently."

She looked at me in horror.

"No way," she answered. "I could never do that."

"Are you sure?" I asked. "Cause if you don't, he's going to be knocking on your door again later today."

She cringed. "I can't tell a lonely old man not to come over."

"Why not?" I countered. "You're not his caretaker. And he is overstepping the bounds."

Finally, she ate her magic mint and walked down the hall. "Hi Nick," she greeted her neighbor. "I need to tell you something. I know when you first moved here, I invited you over for coffee, but the truth is I'm finding your visits stressful. I'm glad to be your neighbor, but I don't want you to knock on my door anymore."

As she spoke these words, her palms began to sweat and a guilty prickle spread over the back of her neck. How could she do this to him? How could she face him in the hallway or the elevator after she'd said these words? What if he told people she was rude, or even cruel?

She'd have to lock herself in her condo and never go out again!

But at the same time these fears and worries were running through her mind, she felt a simultaneous lifting of the resentment she'd been carrying around. Her anger melted away. Asserting her boundary restored her to her highest self and allowed her to feel compassion again. As the old man apologized for coming over too much, she felt her heart soften.

"Thanks for understanding," she responded. "If I am feeling social, I'll knock on *your* door and let you know."

Ever since that experience, my friend has become an expert at setting boundaries. When somebody drops by her condo, she chats with them for as long as she wants, then lets them know when it's time to leave. She has learned to be okay with the fact that people sometimes feel disappointed when she's too busy to hang out, or when she's not feeling social. She has even come to embrace more serious forms of awkwardness, like navigating a dispute over parking spots at her building. Embracing awkwardness gave her a sense of ease and confidence she could never get through avoidance, and she now looks forward to chances to practice that skill.

I love Prentiss Hemphill's definition of boundaries: "Boundaries are the distance at which I can love you and me simultaneously." As long as my friend had no boundaries with the old man, she couldn't love him, and was even starting to hate him. But when she told him what she wanted and needed, her heart opened again. She still chose not to interact with him very often, but she didn't go around with a burning feeling of resentment toward him. And when she did greet him on the stairs or ask how his day was going, she really meant it. Setting boundaries had restored her ability to be sincere.

The Sooner the Better

I have another friend who is a mom, a wife, and a business owner with a wonderful marriage to a great guy. From the beginning, however, she and her in-laws had very different views on parenthood and relationships. Her in-laws were Irish Catholic, while she was drawn to yoga and meditation. For a long time, she kept the peace, thinking their differences weren't a big deal. But when she and her partner wanted to start a family, her mother-in-law made it clear that she would be involved in all things baby, setting up a boundary showdown.

The problems began on the day my friend announced her pregnancy. "*I'm* going to be a grandma!" her mother-in-law declared. "You'll call the baby Patrick, of course, if it's a boy, and Mary if it's a girl."

You can imagine her mother-in-law's displeasure when my friend informed her that the names she and her husband were considering included Aura, River, and Harper, regardless of the baby's sex!

Becoming a new parent involves a steep learning curve. On top of that, fielding unwanted advice about how to raise her child was the last thing my friend wanted, especially because it was coming from someone with a fundamentally different set of values from her own. Because she hadn't set boundaries for her in-laws at the start of their relationship, doing it around issues of parenting now felt impossible. Not wanting to drive a wedge in the family, she bottled up her true feelings and opinions, and they began to eat at her from inside. She felt irritable and prickly, and the affection and appreciation she had for her in-laws was quickly overshadowed by dark feelings of resentment.

When these feelings became too much to bear, my friend decided to set a boundary. In a moment of anger, she informed her mother-in-law that she and her husband had decided to go with a New Age baby blessing instead of a traditional Catholic baptism, and if her mother-in-law didn't *bleeping* like it, she could *bleep* off. This news was devastating to her mother-in-law, and the angry way it was delivered certainly didn't help. Establishing boundaries this late in the game meant there was more pain, broken trust, and hurt feelings on all sides. It took a long time to mend the rift, and my friend experienced deep regret, wishing she had been clear about her boundaries early on. Sure, it would have been uncomfortable then as well, but it would have saved everyone a lot of heartache.

I used to have a friend who was constantly broadcasting my business to the world. Whenever I confided in her, she immediately told our mutual friends what I'd said. She didn't mean any harm, and didn't even realize her behavior bothered me. I told myself she had good intentions, and didn't speak up about how violated I felt whenever she passed along a story, a plan, or a nugget of personal information that was intended for her ears only.

One day, I invited her to attend one of my online healing circles, along with several other friends and clients. In the middle of the circle, she blurted out: "Guess what Adelfa's next project is!" She then revealed what I'd been working on, and encouraged everyone in the circle to congratulate me. I smiled through the deep cringe I felt inside, and accepted everyone's congratulations. As angry as I felt, I knew I had never drawn a line on her oversharing—not when she texted our friends about conversations I'd assumed to be private, and not when she shared my weekend plans with people who had no business knowing them.

After the healing circle, I sent my friend a voice note saying:

Hey, I know you meant to have me celebrated, but sharing something that feels personal isn't cool. It's also not the first time this has happened. I've kept putting your good intentions at the forefront—but this shit sucks, man. I'm going to need you to keep my name outta your mouth for a while. I don't mean this in a fighting-words kind of way, but more like, please respect that if I took time to share things with you, it was meant to be kept with you, not shared without my permission. I don't vibe with that.

This didn't go well. My friend was furious that I hadn't said anything sooner. Even worse, she felt I'd been lying to her—pretending everything was okay between us, while secretly resenting her. She even accused me of setting an impossible number of criteria on our being friends. After calming myself down, I realized that we were coming from different places. I gave her some space to process my request. Unfortunately, she couldn't hold it down. She continued to discuss me and my life (and not in a good way, now that she was pissed!) and I eventually had to dead the friendship.

Unfortunately, this type of situation is common. Most of us don't want to ruffle other people's feathers, so we go along to get along, hoping it will all blow over. We treat boundaries as a radical, last ditch, scary way to deal with a problem that's gotten out of control, not as a way to prevent problems from building up in the first place. We're like high school students putting off a big homework assignment until the hour before it's due. So we end up rushing things or doing them sloppily, and stressing ourselves out in the process. Establishing boundaries early saves everyone a lot of trouble down the road.

Boundary Bloopers

Waiting too long to set boundaries has got to be the #1 boundary blooper, but it's not the only one. Here are some other common mistakes:

Apologizing for boundaries or feeling guilty about them. Have you ever gotten up the courage to set a boundary, only to immediately apologize for it? A friend of mine told a coworker who constantly spoke over her: "Would you mind not interrupting me when I'm talking? Sorry, it's just that I lose my train of thought so easily." Let's be real here. The problem wasn't that she lost her train of thought. The problem was that he interrupted her every five seconds! When we undermine our own boundaries like this, we signal to others that they can keep doing whatever they want, because it's really our problem anyway. Always ask yourself if others are giving as much care and thought to *your* needs as you are to theirs. You may find that you've already stretched your boundaries much further than you intended.

Shifting boundaries under pressure. Have you ever set a boundary, only to let somone badger you into changing it? Like my friend who asked her boyfriend not to let his alcoholic brother move in with them, only to shift that boundary when he begged and pleaded. Sure enough, after a few days, the house was a total mess and my friend was considering ending the relationship. Or the recently married teacher whose mom and sister constantly violated her boundaries by asking for money, even though they knew she and her husband were saving to buy a new home and start a family. When her mother cried and accused her of being cold-hearted, she wavered. And guess what? By the time the couple's baby arrived, *both* the mother and sister had moved into their house uninvited—just when they most needed to feel safe and relaxed. When this began to impact her child, she regretted having caved, no matter how much pressure she was under.

Failing to reevaluate boundaries when appropriate. To be sure, there is a time and a place for reevaluating your boundaries. I once worked with a client who had set strict boundaries with her father, who had abused drugs when she was a child. Now she had a four-year-old daughter whom she refused to let her father see, although he'd been sober for many years, because she didn't want her to be exposed to the same emotional chaos she had endured as a child. When she acknowledged her dad's efforts to get clean and the real changes he'd made in his life, she began to feel more compassion for him and realized that, by holding on to her past hurt, she was foreclosing the possibility of her daughter enjoying this better version of him. So she altered her boundary and allowed her dad to have visits with her daughter, which she supervised.

Failing to establish consequences for boundary violations. The first time my friend's son stole money from her purse, she told him never to do it again. The next time he did it, she complained, but didn't follow up with any consequences. She assumed that shame and disapproval would be a strong enough deterrent, but the pilfering continued. In fact, her son didn't stop stealing until she told him he would have to move out immediately if he ever did it again—a consequence that had real significance to him. Although for most people, the mere fact of being informed of a boundary is enough to keep them from crossing it, others may simply ignore your boundaries.

And unless you are prepared with meaningful consequences, they will gladly continue to violate them. When this happens, spend some time brainstorming consequences—calling the police, cutting off financial support, ending a friendship, or leaving a relationship. These may sound like drastic measures, but they are appropriate responses to serious boundary violations, and they deserve a place in your toolbox.

Explaining or justifying boundaries. When dealing with family or friends, it makes sense to explain or justify your boundaries. After all, when everyone understands exactly why a boundary is being set, it can avoid hurt feelings. The sister of a client of mine had been hoping to use her car to move to a new home in a different state. But the car was old and in need of repair, and my client was concerned that a long road trip would seriously shorten its lifespan. So she told her sister that she didn't feel comfortable lending her the car, and she took a great deal of care in explaining why, sticking to her boundary regardless of her sister's disappointment. The sister understood.

Enabling boundary abusers. On the other hand, when boundary problems arise with people who have taken advantage of you in the past, the less you explain your boundaries, the better. Boundary abusers love it when you explain, because it gives them an opportunity to challenge you or negotiate with you. "You don't want me to come over because you're working from home? Okay, fine. I'll come after you get off work." In cases like this, it's better to simply state your boundaries and leave it at that. You don't owe an explanation to anybody, and certainly not to people who have taken advantage of you in the past.

Boundary-Setting Scripts

If you're not used to setting boundaries, it can be hard to think of what to say. Or worse, you may feel so anxious about protecting others' feelings that you end up saying something vague and confusing, like: "Heeeey, I was wondering if, you know, I'm really busy right now, so . . ." Or: "Just so you know, it's kind of . . . yeah . . . when you do that thing, I . . . you know what I mean?"

To avoid this problem, be sure to clearly identify your boundary for yourself before you try to state it. You can even practice saying it out loud. In my coaching work, I practice boundary-setting scripts with my clients all the time. You can also find these on the Internet, or you can come up with your own. Here are some examples:

Friendly boundary

* "You can crash at my place for two nights, but after that I need my hermit cave to myself."

* "I can dog-sit your husky for the weekend, but I am not scooping any poop."

Boundary + validation

* "I understand you feel strongly about this, but I'm not prepared to change my mind."

* "I know you're disappointed, but I've already decided to send my child to the daycare near my work, not the one at your church."

Boundary + consequence

* "If you show up at my house again, I will call the police."

* "If you grab my arm again, I will end the relationship."

Stone-cold boundary

* "I don't like being teased about my accent."

* "Don't park your SUV on my lawn."

As you can see from these examples, stating a boundary doesn't have to be elaborate or sophisticated. In fact, the simpler and more direct, the better. After all, you want the other person to understand exactly where the line is, with no room for misinterpretation.

A boundary can be stated in a friendly and light-hearted way, or with stone-cold firmness. Only you can determine the appropriate tone. Most important, remind yourself that *boundaries aren't bad*. They exist to prevent conflict and maximize happiness, and this is a good thing for everyone, not just for you.

The Benefits of Boundaries

Good boundaries free you to be kinder, more generous, and more present, because you're not in constant fear of being asked to give more than you want to give. They allow you to enjoy your life and truly love the people around you, because your energy is not tied up in guarding yourself from unwanted intrusions. Boundaries help you to experience less resentment and anxiety, and more joy. When you're good at setting boundaries, people come to understand that you are sincere, and they don't have to guess your true needs, wants, and intentions. They know that, when you offer something, you mean it. This paves the way to better friendships, more stable partnerships, and healthier relationships in general. Finally, boundaries create domains in which you can practice getting comfortable with discomfort. Sometimes they are a bitch, but with enough practice, boundaries can be beautiful.

Try This:

* Come up with scripts for low-risk boundary setting to build your skills. Correct someone who gets your name wrong. Ask neighbors to turn down their music after a certain time. Get clear with your partner or kids about chores. Pick something that's *not* yet out of control or painful so you can establish small victories and get comfortable with the process.

* If you've waited too long to establish boundaries about something, research scripts and tips for difficult conversations. Know that your relationships may get harder in the short term, but that both parties can move toward repair and build something stronger in the long run.

* Review your boundaries with yourself. Do you have a commitment you've made with yourself about reducing harmful behaviors? Do you trust yourself to do what you say? When you build integrity internally, it will flow out into how others treat you.

Chapter 7

Get Your Gratitude On

Last year, a close friend of mine was struggling with depression. Her therapist recommended she start a gratitude journal to boost her mood and appreciate the positive elements of her day-to-day experience. Night after night, my friend did her homework. No matter how much she had cried that day, she dutifully racked her brain for at least three things to put on her gratitude list. Sometimes it took her two hours to come up with three things she was grateful for; sometimes she couldn't think of anything. She came to dread the moment every evening when she had to face her gratitude journal. Not surprisingly, her gratitude practice felt fake, forced, and counterproductive. The more she struggled to come up with items for her list, the more hopeless she felt.

"I don't understand what I'm doing wrong," she told me. "There's all this research saying gratitude makes you happy, but I'm getting more and more stressed out."

The truth is that she didn't feel very grateful. She was depressed, after all, and even when she managed to think of a few things to write on her list, she felt as if she were lying. For example, one day she wrote down that she was grateful for coffee. But when she'd drunk her coffee that morning, she hadn't really felt any gratitude. She'd forced it down with the goal of waking herself up enough to do her job. Her relationship to coffee wasn't so much about gratitude as expedience. But she was *supposed* to be grateful for things, so she put it on her list.

Not only did my friend have a hard time thinking of things to write in her gratitude journal, but her lack of spontaneous gratitude made her wonder if there was something seriously wrong with her. Did everyone else float through the day on a fluffy pink cloud, feeling warm and fuzzy and thankful for everything? Was she some kind of ungrateful freak, an ogre of discontent? Was that why she was depressed? She began to spiral into self-loathing, convinced that her struggles with gratitude were indicative of some deep flaw in her personality.

My friend's story struck a chord with me. Just like her, I've had my own struggles with the so-called "gratitude movement." Does anybody actually enjoy those moments in yoga class or at Thanksgiving dinner when everyone is required to say what they're grateful for? So often, the answers we give are polite and Pollyanna-ish. They come from our heads, not from an innate feeling of thankfulness in our bodies. We're like school children, eager to give the right answer and get an A+ on our gratitude assignment. But how often have you felt that expressing gratitude is a chore, or a well-meant but empty gesture?

And then there are the helpful slogans plastered on bumper stickers and coffee mugs—"Be grateful for every breath," and so forth. Be grateful for every breath? I mean, come on. Who the hell is grateful for literally every breath? And who are these people writing these bumper stickers anyway? Shouldn't they be dealing with their own lives instead of telling everyone else how to feel and what to do?

Even though research tells us that gratitude does wonderful things to the brain, lighting up neural pathways linked to reward and boosting our serotonin, conventional gratitude practices can sometimes leave us feeling grey. If you're like my friend, you may end up *thinking* about gratitude instead of *feeling* it—which explains why those magical benefits have been so elusive. You may put a ton of effort into becoming a gratitude genius—a whiz at making lists, but stuck in your head—when what you want to be doing is luxuriating in actual feelings of gratitude.

The Gratitude Mindset

We've all read the research. Gratitude improves sleep. It reduces depression. It increases happiness and helps us make friends. While scientists are still working to uncover the actual physiological effects of gratitude, there is evidence that gratitude nudges us to live in the medial prefrontal cortex—the part of the brain associated with pleasure. When done effectively, gratitude practices direct our attention away from negative memories, sensations, and experiences, and encourage us to focus on positive ones, with the result that our baseline feelings of happiness and security increase. In other words, we're so busy feeling good things that we forget about all the bad things we meant to think about!

Yet despite this amazing research, and our own best attempts to practice gratitude, we often find ourselves stymied. Think of the last time you got a present you didn't really like. Maybe it was a gift basket from your job, with the waxed fruit and weird little jams and tons and tons of that crinkly paper stuff. You probably said thank you, and maybe even made a dutiful note in your gratitude journal like: "I am grateful to be appreciated by my coworkers." But I'm going to guess you didn't actually *feel* much. All that dopamine and serotonin the research talks about? Nowhere to be found.

Now think of the last time you had a truly great conversation with your best friend. The ideas were flowing, you were laughing, your minds were melding, and you could've talked all night. Your body and mind probably felt great—relaxed, at ease, imbued with happiness. I'm going to guess you didn't waste a bunch of mental energy rehearsing what you were going to say, or worrying about how your best friend was going to react. When you're in a state of joyful connection, your desire to control falls away and your trust in life is massively increased. Now, guess what? Any time you feel that state of joyful connection, *that's gratitude.*

If you've seen too many gratitude bumper stickers, you may start to feel as if gratitude is something "out there"—something you have to search for and think about. But when you shift your mindset to focus on present-moment experiences, you realize that gratitude is right here in the everyday moments when you feel a spontaneous sense of enjoyment, connection, and joyful reciprocity. It's in the giving and receiving of kindness with the people around you.

Gratitude isn't about forcing yourself to think "I am grateful for my dog." It's that big smile and open-hearted feeling you have when your puppy licks your face. It's not telling yourself you need to send someone a thank-you card. It's the feeling of true tenderness you experience when you sincerely reflect on how another human being has impacted your life. It's not an *I should;* it's an *I already do.* When you make the shift from overthinking the practice to deepening it through presence, it becomes easy to recognize moments of gratitude when they occur—no journal required.

Deepen Your Gratitude Practice

The first step to deepening your gratitude practice is simply to start noticing any little interaction that brightens your day, no matter how fleeting or insignificant it may seem. And yes, I am talking about *interactions*—with other human beings—rather than objects, experiences, or moments of beauty. Even though you may feel moved by the sight of a snowy branch or the taste of apple pie, the easiest way to develop those yummy currents of gratitude is to start noticing every time another person is kind to you. Did your neighbor move your packages onto the porch so they wouldn't get wet? Did somebody hold the door for you when you were going into the library? Notice how those moments feel in your body; pay attention to them. This is the beginning of gratitude.

There's no need to write these moments down, or to record them in any way. The point is not to *think* about them, but to *experience* them as they are happening, and to notice yourself enjoying them. The moment you notice that another person is being kind, that is the moment you experience gratitude. And the moment you experience a desire to return that kindness, that is when the magic of gratitude really starts to flow.

The more you practice noticing kindness, the more it starts to appear in your life. You begin to realize how much goodwill is constantly flowing your way. This awareness helps you trust in life, instead of trying to control it. When you become skilled at noticing and receiving kindness, you don't need to worry so much about looking or acting the right way, or saying the right things. When you exist in a state of gratitude, you don't need to get so upset when the events in your life don't turn out exactly as you planned.

I remember working with a client around Thanksgiving a few years back. She was prepping for the celebration and looking forward to seeing some family members she hadn't seen for a long time. She spent the days leading up to the visit cooking up a feast, but as the long-awaited afternoon approached, she began receiving messages from family members saying they couldn't make it to dinner or had to leave earlier than expected. With dinner a few hours away, the celebration went from a party of seven to a party of two—my client and her eight-year-old son.

Frustrated to the point of tears, she wondered how this long-awaited event had turned into such a disaster. Feelings of hurt and disappointment rolled through her in waves. In that moment, she wasn't feeling much gratitude at all. As she sat in the kitchen, her phone crammed with apologetic texts, her son came and sat down beside her. She smiled at him, appreciating the small act of kindness and solidarity. She read over the text messages again and, this time, she realized how sincere they were. Her family wasn't blowing her off. On the contrary, they were concerned with how she felt.

Just moments before, she'd been feeling lonesome and infuriated, but as she connected to the tiny threads of kindness running through the experience, her tunnel vision expanded into a bigger picture of reality—a reality in which she was loved, appreciated, and surrounded by kind people, even if this dinner was going to be smaller than she'd planned. What could've been a profoundly disappointing experience contained seeds of warmth, connection, and gratitude.

Half an hour later, my client's stepdaughter, who had texted to apologize that she couldn't stay for more than an hour, called back to say that her plans had changed and she could stay for the entire evening. Shortly after that, an aunt who had been out of touch for years (and hadn't been invited to the holiday dinner) called to ask if she could stop by. And before my client knew it, her perfect party of two was restored to a perfect party of seven.

The important lesson here is that this woman was able to shift her attention from what she lacked to what filled her life with joy. Her genuine sense of enjoyment in things as they were calmed her enough so she could cope with the situation. In the end, what was most memorable for her about the evening wasn't the dinner or the company; it was her ability to work herself out of her own frustration by noticing the kindness that surrounded her, even when her plans went awry.

Another client of mine was struggling with social anxiety. Whenever she went to a party, she only noticed what felt bad—the painfully loud music, the overwhelming crush of bodies, the fear that she'd say or do the wrong thing. She barely even noticed when the host hung up her coat for her, or when the bartender kindly mixed a non-alcoholic drink, or when strangers tried to set her at ease by engaging her in conversation. She was filtering out the positive interactions, and focusing on the things she found distressing. I challenged her to notice every act of kindness that occurred when she went to a party, and to acknowledge it out loud: "It's so kind of you to take my coat." "It's so kind of you to make me a such a beautiful drink."

The simple act of thanking strangers for their kindness activated something inside my client's heart. Suddenly, she could feel a warm current of gratitude connecting her to these people. She found herself smiling more, engaging in more meaningful conversations, and making more friends. Things that used to bother her, like the loud music and worries about what she was going to say, began to fade away. Her newfound connection to gratitude was changing her life.

Gratitude Everywhere

Once you've developed your skills to recognize moments of gratitude in your interactions with others, you'll find it easier to notice gratitude everywhere. A friend of mine was an experienced mushroom hunter who loved nothing more than to spend hours in the woods looking for her favorite varieties of edible fungi. Every time she spotted a patch of her favorite mushroom "friends," it felt like running into one of her human friends. She experienced that same surge of joy and recognition. She felt tenderness toward these wonderful organisms and did her best to treat them with care and respect. Although she didn't realize it at the time, her relationship with mushrooms was characterized by a great deal of gratitude, which explains why it brought her so much happiness.

Whenever you treat an element of the universe with respect, kindness, tenderness, or some other form of positive engagement, you are effectively practicing gratitude. When you enjoy a piece of cake, or a piece of artwork, or the sound of music, that's gratitude. Personally, I've come to realize that my practice of taking photos is a form of gratitude. I see a beautiful tree or a butterfly, and I honor that moment by snapping a picture of it on my smart phone. I also keep a gratitude journal, but I do love having an entire album of these photos, reminding me of the joy and beauty that surrounds me. Some of my coaching clients practice gratitude by helping others, smiling at strangers, dancing and singing—anything that puts them in touch with the flow of life and contributes to the river of kindness.

Gifts of Gratitude

Connecting with gratitude can snap you back into a positive mindset when you find yourself in situations you either fear or dislike. It can help you enjoy what *is* and lead you to discover hidden gems in the most unexpected places. And when you develop your capacity to enjoy what *is*, you automatically start to share that gift with others. We've all met people who seem preternaturally peaceful, joyful, and at ease—people who just keep glowing while everyone else is freaking out. What's their secret? No, it's not that they're trying harder to be happy or living in blissful oblivion. It's that they've taught themselves to truly enjoy and appreciate their lives, moment by moment, whether things are going their way or not.

Gratitude strengthens social ties and promotes healthy exchanges. It brings us closer to our neighbors, teachers, friends, and families. It's not about sitting in your room alone trying to make the perfect list; it's about engaging in the dance of life. When you express gratitude, you ignite happiness within your being, and you share that happiness with the people around you. When you return kindness, you double down on the kindness that was originally given to you. When you expand your capacity for enjoyment, you can appreciate even difficult events. And the more you enjoy your life, the less you need to control it obsessively. Now *that* sounds like a sweet gift.

Try This:

* Train yourself to notice kindness in others. The next time somebody does you a small favor, try saying: "That was kind of you." This simple act of appreciation will make you even more likely to notice kindness in the future. If you want to take it to the next level, you can write a gratitude letter or e-mail, send a text, or thank that person publicly on social media.

* The next time you're in a difficult situation, take a moment to connect with even one small element of kindness, beauty, or appreciation. This will pop you out of your tunnel vision and help you see the bigger picture.

* If a conventional gratitude journal isn't working for you, try a photo journal, a sketchbook, or a little altar where you can place objects that mean something to you. The important part isn't the form your gratitude takes; it's the emotions you cultivate when you appreciate your life.

Chapter 8

Journal Up

I have a close friend who carries a shiny red notebook with her everywhere. When we meet up for coffee, if she gets there first, I always find her writing while she waits for me. She writes on the subway, or when she is waiting for a doctor's appointment, or in any other little window of time when most people would be playing with their phones. One day I told her: "I love your commitment to that thing."

The way her eyes beamed reminded me of parents who can't wait to show you pictures of their new baby. It was as if she'd been waiting for me to ask about her little red pal the entire time.

"You have no idea, Adelfa. This journal has changed my life."

She explained to me that journals aren't just for high school girls with crushes, or for people who think "live, laugh, love" is a profound and original slogan. Journaling is also for grown-ass women who know their own minds—or would like to know their own minds, anyway. She explained that, even though she was shy and quiet in her everyday life, the version of herself that came out in the red notebook always felt raw, authentic, and like her most genuine self. Whenever she had a problem, she holed up with her notebook for an hour or two and, when she was finished, she always knew the right thing to do.

"This is why I love my journal," she claimed. "Because no matter how overwhelmed or distraught I feel when I start writing, I know I'm perfectly safe. Nobody's going to jump off the page and judge me or tell me what I'm doing wrong. By the time I'm done writing, I usually feel much stronger."

When my next birthday came around, she surprised me with a big red notebook of my own, along with a card that read:

Happy birthday, Adelfa. Leos deserve the biggest and shiniest notebook at the stationary store. Get ready for your life to change. I love you!

The next morning, I decided to give it a try. I set a timer for twenty minutes, then sat down with my shiny new notebook. "Okay," I thought to myself. "Let's see what this is all about!" I picked up a pen and wrote . . . this:

This is stupid. I don't even know what I'm supposed to be writing about. The hell with this. I don't want to. I really don't even want to. I could be doing something else. I hate this. What if someone reads this? I shouldn't write important things in here, just in case. God, I wish the timer would go off. Fuuuuuuckkkkk!

I wasn't sure who I was supposed to be on the page. Was I supposed to be somber and formal? Funny? Professional? How did people get past the awkward first paragraphs and into a state of flow?

I almost stopped right then and put the notebook away. But then I thought of how badly I would feel if my friend came over in a few months and saw that it was blank. I put my pen back on the page and tried again:

Okay, honestly, what's really going on is I'm scared I don't have the strength to deal with the feelings that may come up if I write in here. And it would be easier not to write at all than to run the risk of being overwhelmed by my own stupid feelings and then disappointed that I don't know what to do next.

The moment I started writing about what I was really thinking and feeling, the magic started to happen.

I stopped worrying about sounding dumb, and started to feel curious about this human being who was telling me her thoughts in such an honest, unguarded way. When the timer went off, I ignored it and kept writing. It felt a little scary, but also extremely exciting to write down thoughts that had only ever existed in the confines of my mind. It was the writing equivalent of dancing when you're home alone with the music blasting. I found myself intentionally writing down the thoughts that scared me just to see how it felt. (Spoiler alert: It felt amazing!) When I finished writing, I called my friend. "I think I get it," I admitted. She laughed and answered: "Welcome to the cult."

Why Journaling?

Your journal is a safe space where you can pour out your heart, uninterrupted and without fear of being bombarded with unwanted advice. If you're a person who worries about burdening others, a journal can be a great companion, because you never have to fear that you've rambled on about your problems for too long. For many of us, this kind of freedom can have tremendous healing benefits.

A friend of mine told me about a beautiful practice she had done in an AA meeting. Members in the meeting were allowed to speak about whatever was on their minds and hearts for three solid minutes. The rule was that no one in the audience was allowed to say anything in response—no advice, no thoughts, no apologies, no empathy, no relating, *nothing.* "You should've seen the things people were unleashing because they knew they didn't have to hear someone else speak about it once they were done. It's as if they were happy to leave their shit on the table and walk away from it. It was magical, Adelfa," she marveled. While I've never been to an AA meeting, I did relate to the feeling of leaving it all on the table and freely walking away. It was the same feeling I got when I wrote in my journal.

Writing is a way to have a conversation with the part of yourself that's most authentic. Often, that also happens to be the part of you that is the wisest, most compassionate, most creative, and most courageous. But don't take my word for it. This shit has been scientifically proven. In a study of the amygdala that combined Buddhist teachings with modern neuroscience, one psychologist found that putting feelings into words made sadness, anger, and pain less intense.[1] Another study done at Michigan State University uncovered neural evidence that expressive writing frees up cognitive resources—in other words, the simple act of writing down worries releases some of the burden on the brain.[2]

Have you ever tried to carry too many objects at once? Groceries in one arm, library books in the other, your kid's hockey equipment slung over one shoulder, your actual kid on your back because his shoes hurt, the offending shoes in your hand . . . you get the idea. When you carry too many objects at once, your mental and physical states can be overwhelmed. The same is true when you carry a lot in your mind. This may include heavy items like past trauma or abuse that is difficult to share verbally, or a combination of lighter things—a job, a relationship, a friend in the hospital, a need to pay the bills. All these burdens can work together to weigh you down and stress you out. Writing is a way to put down some of these burdens so you can deal with them in a sane and reasonable way.

A final study I read found that when you keep a journal, you can better organize events in your mind because it helps you make sense of trauma and recall situations more accurately, thus improving your working memory.[3] The act of writing allows the development of what's called a "coherent narrative" of life. In other words, it takes the events you experience and integrates them into your overall perspective. The more time you spend with your journal, the less random, scary, and unpredictable life feels, and the more it starts to make sense. Your journal helps weave the events of your life into a single, highly meaningful story, and can make you far less depressed and anxious in the process.

I now have no idea how I used to get through the day without my writing ritual. Now I feel as lost without my notebook as I would if I left home without my cell phone. I turn to my red notebook multiple times a day, checking in about how I feel physically and emotionally. If I'm feeling nervous before a big event or an important social interaction, I spend five or ten minutes with my notebook. The act of writing always clears my mind. I can also flip through the pages and look back over all the *other* times I've felt nervous, and remind myself that they turned out okay. My journal functions as an external hard drive, storing facts I wouldn't necessarily remember myself, especially in a moment of crisis or when feeling overwhelmed. It reminds me that my higher self is right there, within me, every time I need to access her, restoring emotional balance whenever something threatens to knock me off course.

Getting Started with Journaling

First, buy yourself a big red notebook. Okay, fine, it doesn't have to be red. Get whatever color you like. It can be lined or unlined, thick or thin. The important thing is that it must not have the words "live, laugh, love" printed on it *anywhere*.

Next, get started by answering one of the following prompts:

* One thing I've never told anybody is . . .

* I've never confessed how I really feel about . . .

* I am afraid to even let myself think about . . .

* I wonder what would happen if I finally let myself . . .

* I've always assumed _____, but lately I've been wondering if _____ is more accurate.

* One lie I need to stop telling myself is . . .

* If I weren't so _____, I would _____ . . .

If these questions remind you of those icebreaker games you played the one time you tried speed-dating, that's because they serve the same function. They cut through the awkward small-talk and get straight to the juicy stuff. These prompts can help you get into the habit of being honest, brave, and vulnerable on the page, which massively increases the likelihood that you will strike gold.

What do I mean by striking gold? I mean those moments when you stumble across an unexpected insight, a new idea, or a newfound sense of compassion for yourself or somebody else. The longer you work with your own writing ritual, the more frequently you will find this kind of gold, and the more you will treasure your writing time.

A client of mine was having a hard time letting herself write down honest answers to these questions. She was a kind, virtuous person and she was afraid that, if she even tried to answer the prompts, she would discover a nasty, ungrateful, out-of-control harpy lurking just beneath the surface. She had been abused as a child, and had worked hard to surround herself with love and light as an adult. What if she uncovered a well of trauma that she was not prepared to handle? What if, instead of a wise and compassionate higher self, she discovered an angry self, a wounded self, or a self nobody would like, even her?

We decided that, instead of answering the prompts right away, she would start by simply writing about the fears the prompts were evoking. Over the course of a week, she wrote page after page about her fear of being unloved if she revealed any negative emotions. She wrote about her belief that she had to walk a tightrope of extreme "goodness" to avoid being overwhelmed by feelings of shame and panic. She wrote about how she'd developed a strategy of being meticulously "good" to avoid her parents' anger as a child. Finally, she mourned the fact that this extreme concern with proper behavior made her overly formal and stilted in social interactions, and prevented her from letting out the goofy, wild side that only came out around her closest and most trusted friends.

When she showed up for her next session, she apologized profusely. "Adelfa, I didn't manage to answer the prompts. I'm sorry for letting you down. It was just too scary."

But when she showed me what she'd written, I couldn't help grinning. "You *did* answer the prompts," I assured her. "You answered every single one of them, by writing honestly about why it was too hard to answer them or even think about them. You're off to a great start."

After that, she started writing in her notebook every day. She realized that the biggest thing she was avoiding wasn't some repressed inner demon; it was acknowledging the fact that fear controlled her every decision and behavior. She began to take note of her fears, which usually took the form of "Nobody will like me if I . . . ." Putting these fears on the page, where she could see them all at once, helped her to see how arbitrary they were. After all, most of her friends indulged in the same behaviors that she would consider unacceptable if she engaged in them herself—for example, laughing too loudly, talking too much, occasionally showing up late, or canceling a plan. If she could like and love her friends who did these very human things, why did she need to hold herself to a different standard?

Another client enjoyed working with the prompts so much that she returned to them again and again, checking in with them every month to explore her personal truth on a deep level. The prompts forced her to home in on her true feelings and desires, and helped her to articulate clear statements about who she was and what she wanted. For example: "If I wasn't afraid of my family's judgment, I would quit this job and spend a year doing volunteer work abroad." These statements became a guiding force in her life, and she reread them frequently, especially when she had to make a big decision. Working with her journal helped her bring her *truest* self to the surface, and manifest that self every day.

Revise Your Life Story

One of my favorite ways to work with journals is to challenge my clients to revise or even rewrite a story they've been telling about their lives. For example, one of my clients had the following story:

> My sister and I were neglected as children. Our parents would leave us alone in the house for entire days at an age when most kids still had babysitters. Nobody made me a lunch to take to school, and I often went hungry. My whole life, I've fended for myself, and I learned at an early age that I can't rely on other people for anything.

Now, I want to emphasize that there is nothing wrong with this story. It's true; it's accurate; the events in question really happened. When I talk about revising your life story, I don't mean changing the facts or denying the traumas. I mean using that same set of facts to explain your strengths instead of your weaknesses, your growth instead of your "stuckness."

Revising your life story is not about throwing sparkles and glitter over terrible events. It's about uncovering hidden gems you may have missed over years of telling your story in the same way every time. Here's what my client came up with after a few tries:

> Rightly or wrongly, my sister and I were given a great deal of freedom and independence from a young age. We learned to be resourceful and take care of ourselves, and I think this explains why I've always done well at my jobs. When a problem comes up, I'm not afraid to tackle it, and I don't expect other people to fix things for me. I have many skills other people lack, because I'm not afraid of learning.

My client had been resistant to doing this exercise—after all, her childhood had been difficult, and she didn't want to let her parents off the hook for their neglect. But as soon as she'd written down her new story, a look of wonder spread over her face. "It feels like a burden has lifted," she told me. "This is still my story, but there's so much light inside of it."

Without denying the difficulty, she had found something of value in her experience. Not only that, but there was something powerful about claiming the benefits of her upbringing, not just the damage. While she may have been the victim of a shipwreck, she did swim away with some treasures, and this exercise helped her notice and value that fact. Now, when strangers ask about her childhood, she tells them some combination of the old and new stories. Although she was resistant to "denying the truth" of her childhood, she realized this new version felt even more true than the old one, and she felt better when she told it.

Another client used her journal to rewrite the story of a relationship that ended badly. Here's her original story:

> I thought Xavier and I would be together for the rest of our lives. Our first six years together were magical. But in year seven, he started drinking and it changed his whole personality. I stayed around for another three years, foolishly hoping he would change back. I can't believe I wasted so much time, when I could've been moving on.

Here's her revised story:

> Xavier and I spent a magical six years together, exploring our shared love of sailboats and going to lots of music festivals. I loved him so much that, when he developed a drinking problem,

I did everything I could to try to help him. I discovered deep wells of caring and loyalty that kept me going through three difficult years. Ultimately, I learned to give myself the same care and loyalty I'd been giving him, and I succeeded at leaving the relationship.

Instead of beating herself up for being codependent, this client acknowledged the real love and compassion she had given to her partner, qualities she was now learning to embody in a healthy and balanced way. Instead of bemoaning "wasted time," she saw that three years was in fact a perfectly reasonable timeframe for making the huge transformation required of her to be ready to move on.

I can't front; this practice is some powerful shit. No matter how much pain, regret, or grief you have, revising your life story can restore a sense of dignity, pride, and self-compassion. If life has stolen something from you, you can use this practice to take it back—to assert that you haven't been destroyed or erased.

Journaling Hiccups

One client of mine never wrote anything too personal or revealing in her journal because she was worried someone might find it and read it. As a result, her journaling became more of a gratitude and happy-mood narrative, as opposed to a genuine attempt to communicate with her authentic self. This situation could've lasted for months, but one day an incident at her job left her frazzled and upset. When she got home that day, she found herself alone and desperate for an outlet. She picked up her pen and began to let loose in the pages of her notebook, allowing her true and raw self to spill onto the paper. When she set down her pen, she was five pages into a monolog that included her most unfiltered thoughts. The relief she felt as she finished was instantaneous.

This one experience was enough to convince her that being honest in her writing was far better than sticking to safe, nice paragraphs about her day. As she began writing more and more over the coming days, her fear of being exposed through her writing started to wane, replaced by the thrill of expressing herself in an authentic way. Her journaling became an indispensable tool for reflecting on whatever was happening to her and within her. She began to see that the things she had been afraid to write were in fact big road signs pointing the way: "Growth opportunity just ahead!" "This is important; write about me!"

Eventually, she began to look forward to digging into her journal. If she went a day or more without writing, she found that she felt "off." She realized her release on the page gave her greater mental capacity to cope with whatever her day brought. And if she ever found herself holding back because she was afraid of someone reading her notebook, she told herself she could always tear out those pages and throw them away—and occasionally, she did. The important thing wasn't having a permanent record of her most intense thoughts and emotions; it was writing them down at all.

Another client of mine had the opposite problem. She immediately used her little red book to pour out her raw, unfiltered feelings of anxiety about being a new mother. For those who know, people who have just given birth experience a sweet juxtaposition of all the most beautiful feelings you can fathom, paired with sleep deprivation, sore nipples, a healing vagina or belly, and a body recovering from serious trauma. And these stresses were getting to my client. She found herself constantly plagued by worries about her baby, intrusive thoughts about terrible things that could happen, and ruminations about how hard life would be when she had to return to work—the list went on and on.

Writing became her outlet for releasing these worries and fears—and there's nothing wrong with that. The problem arose when she began to focus *exclusively* on these worries, leaving aside the positive aspects of new motherhood. She knew that, when she opened her book, a host of negative feelings and thoughts would pour out of her. Worse yet, she felt guilt and shame when she admitted that she was experiencing these feelings. Her journal became an emotional trash can—an eloquent one, but a trash can nonetheless.

Eventually, she became overwhelmed with disappointment that nothing was being "fixed" by her writing practice. She began to dread opening her notebook, knowing it would mirror back a dark version of herself. When she told me what was happening, we dove in and got curious about what was going on when she sat down to write. And we discovered that her journal pages were the only place where she felt she could voice her true feelings. It was hard to talk to her husband about what she was going through, and writing was her only real release. The only problem was that reading over her own thoughts left her feeling depressed and hopeless. Was her life really as bad as it sounded? Was this really how she wanted to remember the first months of her baby's life?

To remedy this sad situation, we discussed ways to make her writing less stream-of-consciousness and more structured. We came up with a list of prompts that would help her generate positive memories that she would be happy to read about later. While not denying her anxiety and fear, these prompts helped her build up a reserve of hope, pride, and happiness. Now, when she flipped through her journal, she saw a record of good moments interspersed with the worries and ruminations. She saw herself as a new mother who was trying hard and doing her utmost to give the best possible life to her baby. By transforming her writing, she transformed her image of herself—and that's powerful indeed.

Try This:

* If you are used to writing stream-of-consciousness monologs in your notebook, try making a list, answering a prompt, or doing some other structured kind of writing.

* If you are used to only writing lists, answering prompts, or doing some other structured kind of writing, see what happens when you write a stream-of-consciousness monolog.

* Identify a couple of the stories you frequently tell about your life and experiment with rewriting them. How have your most traumatic moments led to your greatest strengths?

* If you catch yourself writing something dishonest in your journal, there is no shame in correcting yourself. Try writing down the true version, then write about why it was hard for you to say that in the first place.

Chapter 9

Take That Breath

Getting cut off in traffic by someone who's not paying attention. Losing your phone or wallet and trying to retrace your steps. Being late to an important meeting or appointment. Having your flight canceled. Getting a terrible grade on a test. Finding out you didn't get the job. Having your phone ping with a break-up text. Have you ever been majorly stressed out by experiences like these, only to have some well-meaning jerk tell you: "Just *b r e a t h e!*"?

You usually hear this obnoxious advice when you are panicked, rushed, or overwhelmed. The last thing you want to do is to pause and take a deep breath. And the first thing you want to do is put your foot on the neck of the person telling you to do it—preferably while shouting: "*You* just fucking breathe, asshole!"

At the same time, it's undeniable that intentional breathing is the superfood of self-care. Breathing intentionally really can relax your body, reboot your emotions, and restore your ability to respond to situations in a graceful and effective way. The "just breathe" people aren't *wrong;* they're just annoying. But if you train yourself to breathe intentionally, you can beat them to the punch, and enjoy the benefits of intentional breathing minus the smarmy advice.

Intentional Breathing

I think one reason the words "take a deep breath" used to piss me off is that they implied I was hysterical and needed to calm down. How many times are women told to take deep breaths when they're feeling strong emotions, whereas men's emotional reactions are assumed to be totally valid? Can you even *think* of the last time you heard someone tell a man to take a deep breath? Too often, the "take a deep breath" advice feels like a "nice" way of telling a woman her emotions are wrong or too strong, rather than a sincere attempt to help her achieve her own goals. Maybe that woman doesn't *want* to feel different emotions right now; maybe she doesn't *want* to feel them less intensely. So why are people rushing in with the assumption she needs to change?

Nobody appreciates being told to calm down, let alone being told how and when to breathe. But here's the thing they don't tell you about breathing. It's not just for calming you down. It's for powering you up. Yogis, monks, athletes, military personnel, and CEOs all use breathwork to increase their energy, courage, and fortitude, and you can do the same. Intentional breathing isn't just some last-ditch tool you can reach for in a crisis; it's a secret weapon you can use during the most important moments of your life. Want to negotiate a deal? Take that breath. Confront someone who's gotten up in your grill? Take that breath. Free solo El Capitan? That's right—take that breath, and no rock wall can stop you.

If you learn how to use your breath to power up, you're less likely to become panicked or overwhelmed in the first place, and therefore less likely to need intentional breathing to calm down. You can learn to live in a state of strength and balance in which it becomes increasingly difficult for something or someone to ruffle your feathers. You can train your nervous system to exist in a chill and collected state around the clock, so situations that would have left you overwrought in the past barely move your needle. Best of all, once you're well established in an intentional breathing practice, you can tell all those strangers with their patronizing advice where to stick it.

Intentional breathing is something your grown, healing, empowered self can master with some practice. Whenever I feel anxious or overwhelmed, I remind myself that inner peace is only a few breaths away. This gives me the motivation to stop what I'm doing and *breathe*. There are many ways to work with breath. Here's the basic breathwork routine I use in my coaching practice. It's easy to learn, and you can use it as many times as you want. It consists of these three simple steps.

Decide to take a breath. Before you even take an intentional breath, *decide* to take one. Make a statement inside your head or out loud: "I am going to pause and take this breath." This may sound overly subtle, but trust me, it's key. When you make a choice, you take back your power. You assert your will, your values, and your higher self. Even making this tiny choice puts you back in charge and restores your sense of agency. This moment of assertion sends a powerful message to your nervous system, putting you in a mindset of courage and autonomy. If you're in a chaotic situation, it gives you a chance to pause—a split second in which you can regain some degree of mental clarity. If you're surrounded by people who are upset or highly activated, it helps you separate yourself from their anxiety and creates a space in which you can check in with your own emotions.

Take the biggest, baddest breath you can. Inhale as deeply as you would if you were coming up from the bottom of a pool or taking the first hit from a freshly rolled one at the end of the day. Inhale deeply, no matter who's watching. Fuck the short, shallow nonsense for this one minute. This is *your* breath, so take it. Fill your belly with air—all the way—before you exhale. There is no need to rush. When you're ready to exhale, sigh, moan, or make whatever sounds feel right, knowing that they spring from your body's own innate healing wisdom. Studies have shown that sighing reinflates the tiny air sacs in your lungs, which can become depleted through normal breathing. So be sure to take your time, drink in the air, and let yourself enjoy a good sigh while you're at it.

Assume the position. Linking intentional breath to a posture adjustment doubles down on the benefits, because it sends a message to your body that you are strong, confident, and able to handle whatever life is throwing your way. And it sends the same message to the people around you. As you exhale, let your shoulders fall back and make sure you're not sticking your chest out. Allow your chest to open and lift your chin slightly. If you're in the middle of a conversation, argument, negotiation, or other high-stakes interaction, look the other person straight in the eye. If you're alone, smile at yourself and state an affirmation or intention.

I've lost track of the number of times I've paused to take an intentional breath, only to have someone comment on how poised and self-assured I seem. By using all three of these steps, I've breezed through situations that would have capsized me in the past. Nothing makes me happier than watching a client go through this same transformation using this simple technique.

Ya Breath in Action

A client of mine was dealing with a difficult neighbor. He was a real piece of work—one of those people who live to complain. And he expected everyone around him to hop to it whenever he had a beef. My client had already cut down her favorite plum tree because he complained that it was dropping fruit on his lawn, and now he was complaining about the above-ground pool she'd bought for her kids as a reward for their terrific grades that year. When it came to this neighbor, she felt like a small animal with no defenses. Her only strategy was to give him whatever he wanted, regardless of whether it was reasonable. She knew this wasn't a viable long-term plan, but couldn't see what else she could do.

Whenever her neighbor started in on one of his rants, my client felt pressured to give him an answer right away.

Before she even had time to assess how she felt about his demands, she'd say something like: "I'll take care of it." We decided that, the next time she saw this neighbor coming, she would take a deep, intentional breath before he even crossed into her yard. This would build up her power before he was right in her face. If he asked her to make a change or agree to some new rule, she would take a breath before saying *anything*. I reminded her that she had a right to take her time and think things over. There was no law saying she had to agree to anything her neighbor asked for within five seconds.

Sure enough, that weekend when the kids were playing in the pool, the nasty neighbor came over to complain. When she spotted him, she thought to herself: "Okay friend, let's do this." She put down her lemonade and took the biggest, baddest breath of her life. At the end of the breath, she reset her posture, dropped her shoulders back, and tilted her chin up like a queen. She decided to stay in her chair and force him to approach her, instead of jumping up to see what he wanted. Right off the bat, the intentional breath helped her assert her power and dignity, instead of automatically reverting to a submissive role.

By the time the neighbor walked up to her, he was already on the back foot. After all, he was in *her* territory, since she hadn't come to meet him on the boundary line as she normally did. She took another breath. Instead of anxiously asking him what the problem was and how she could help, she waited for him to talk.

"Every time the kids jump in the pool," he complained, "it splashes water onto my lawn."

Was this dude serious? I mean, come on. But this is the kind of thing that would normally have put my client into a tailspin, promising to fix it and swearing it would never happen again.

When she felt the old instinct for immediate appeasement rising up inside her, she managed to tell herself to take a third breath before saying anything. While he stood there waiting, she took a nice long breath in through her nose, then let it out slowly and made one last adjustment to her posture. Then she looked her neighbor straight in the eye and said: "Honestly Frank, that's probably not gonna change."

Boom! It was as if she'd discovered a true superpower. The neighbor looked surprised, and a little impressed, and maybe even a tiny bit scared. "Okay," he mumbled. "Well, I just wanted to let you *know*. Beautiful day out here. Your garden looks great."

Before she knew it, he was shuffling back to his own house without her having agreed to change a single thing. She had held her ground calmly and firmly, and she was stunned to discover that it worked. The intentional breath had bought her enough time to get ahead of her old timid reflexes and make the change she wanted. Instead of provoking conflict with her neighbor, her polite but firm refusal had nipped a potential confrontation in the bud. And instead of feeling anxious and defeated after this interaction, she felt a sense of pride, warmth, and accomplishment. This one interaction rescripted their entire relationship. The neighbor stopped complaining about every little thing, and my client stopped living with constant anxiety. They even had a couple positive exchanges now and then, and became good neighbors if not close friends.

Intentional breathing is powerful shit. It puts you in charge. It restores you to your highest self. It gives you time to get clear and check in with your true needs, desires, and boundaries. Just as important, it sends a clear message to others that you are strong, capable, and not to be fucked with. Humans are sensitive creatures, constantly picking up on subtle physical and emotional cues even when they're not consciously aware of it. When you practice intentional breathing, the people around you can tell that you're in a strong, balanced state, and will respond to you in a different way than if they detect you're anxious, uncertain, and inhibited.

Another client of mine had a goal of learning to surf. Her boyfriend was a surfer (I understood wanting to match that swag!) and they were both excited about the idea of surfing together, instead of her watching him from the shore. The only problem was that she was afraid of waves. She felt fine when they paddled out from the beach, but as soon as they got close to the actual surf break, her heart started beating faster, her breath grew shallow, and she descended into a full-blown panic attack—with her boyfriend "helpfully" reminding her to breathe.

It got to the point where she was almost ready to give up on surfing, even though that prospect disappointed her. She didn't want to miss out on the opportunity to have fun in the ocean just because she was afraid. We decided she would try again, but this time she would incorporate intentional breathing *before* she started getting scared. She would take her first intentional breath while she was standing on the beach, before she even put one toe in the water. While she took this breath, she would say to herself: "I am *choosing* to face the waves."

After paddling halfway to the surf break, she would pause and take another breath, again reminding herself that she was *choosing* to engage with these scary feelings. She let her boyfriend know that under no circumstances was he to tell her when or how to breathe. She could handle all that. (Also, if he tried to tell her how to breathe, she would probably tip him off his board.)

By taking these deep, intentional breaths *before* she got to the surf break, she felt calm and confident when it was time to duck under the waves and find her place in the lineup. She didn't have to panic, because the intentional breathing had cleared out just enough anxiety that she could handle the situation, even though it was new and challenging for her. And when she did get rolled by a big wave, she spontaneously went limp and let the ocean carry her harmlessly back to the surface, where she felt an unexpected surge of confidence and joy. The intentional breathing had sent a message to her nervous system that she was safe, and her body responded by loosening up and taking spontaneous, appropriate action.

It's All About Trust

Because it buys you time, intentional breathing helps you build trust in your own ability to make good decisions and take appropriate actions. If you're always going off half-cocked—agreeing to things you don't really agree with, making decisions when you're overwhelmed and then having to deal with the consequences—your self-confidence may become shaky. But the more you use breathing as a tool, the more likely it is that you will make agreements you're genuinely happy about, and decisions that are truly helpful and effective in achieving your goals. The more you use intentional breathing, the more you can express your authentic self, with the result that your relationships with others become more meaningful, satisfying, and real.

When you're afraid of something, you're more likely to try to control it. Your mind gets caught up in endless rehearsals, and your intuitions get drowned out by the carefully planned scripts you think you need to follow. Intentional breathing reduces your fear, and therefore restores your ability to flow with situations. Think of athletes who trust their bodies to move instinctively to the right part of the field, or musicians who practice for hours but then let go completely when they're on stage. You can't plan out every move in a soccer game, but if you're present and relaxed, you can trust your body to kick that ball into the goal.

My client with the nasty neighbor could never have *planned* to say what she did. It just came out, and it was perfect, because her mind was clear instead of being clogged up with nervous rehearsals. My client who was learning to surf could never have *planned* to go limp and relax the first time she was rolled by a big wave; her certainty that waves were dangerous would have prevented it. But her intentional breathing put her in a place of ease and clarity, so that she was able to follow her intuition instead of being bombarded by not-so-helpful messages from the voices in her head.

There is no doubt in my mind that intentional breathing is magical. Yet despite its many benefits, I've lost track of the number of clients who claim to hate breathwork. Usually, this is because they think they can use intentional breathing to *force* themselves to be calm or peaceful, or have some other "good" emotion, no matter how panicked or upset they're feeling. And what happens when we try to force our emotions to change? The original "bad" emotion doubles down and gets even stronger! The panic says: "Nuh-uh, you're not controlling *me*!" And then it jacks up the volume to eleven. The anxiety says: "Wait a sec, I wasn't finished yet!" And then it makes an even bigger effort to get your attention.

Intentional breathing is not about *forcing* "bad" feelings to go away and magically replacing them with "good" feelings of your own choosing. Rather, it works by creating space in which it is extremely likely that this change will happen. Maybe that sounds subtle, but there's a huge difference there. You're not *forcing* your emotions to change; you're just creating favorable conditions for confidence to appear and anxiety to leave. It's like leaving cookies out for Santa Claus. You can't *force* him to come down the chimney, but you can make it nice and tempting.

Along the same lines, you can't *force* unwanted thoughts and feelings to go away, but you can make it easier for them to leave. As an ancient Chinese philosopher advised: "Build your opponent a golden bridge to retreat across." (This quote is attributed to Sun Tzu, although the original source is debatable.) In other words, if you make it *easy and attractive* for the bad shit to leave, it probably will!

Try This:

* Take a look at your calendar. Do you have any stressful events coming up in the next week or two? A doctor's appointment? A presentation at work? A custody handoff with your ex? Identify how and when you'd like to use your intentional breaths in each of these situations. For example, you may decide to take an intentional breath before you get out of the car, before you enter the room, and before you speak.

* Practice taking an intentional breath when you're having a conversation with a friend or someone you find non-threatening. Get comfortable taking those extra seconds before answering a question or agreeing to a plan. The next time you have to speak with a person you find intimidating, you'll already have plenty of practice at using intentional breathing.

* Practice taking a breath when you're feeling happy and confident, not just when you're anxious or nervous. Taking an intentional breath when you're happy helps those feelings get established in your body, so that a confident, easy mood becomes your baseline.

Chapter 10

Know Your *Why* and Count Your Wins

Imagine that somebody asks you to go into your backyard and dig a giant hole, but offers no further explanation. You'd probably tell them to go find a giant hole and jump in it. But let's say, for the sake of this example, that you agree to do it.

So there you are, digging away with your shovel, your shirt soaked in sweat, likely thinking to yourself how stupid and pointless the job is. After a while, you probably start looking for ways to slack off. Maybe you start digging more slowly, or you scoop up a little less dirt each time, feeling impressed and humbled by the folks who do this kind of work on a daily basis—because, my lord, this shit ain't easy. My guess is that, before long, you'll throw down the shovel and find something else to do.

Sound about right?

Now imagine that somebody tells you there is a diamond buried deep in that same ground, and that you can keep it if you dig it out. The sun is still hot and the shovel's wooden handle still puts splinters in your hands. But suddenly, you don't mind digging for as long as it takes. After all, there's a freaking diamond down there!

We've all known people who have accomplished superhuman feats when they've had a really good reason to do so—a really big diamond at the bottom of the hole. Like my client, a single mom who put herself through nursing school while working full-time so she could give her children a better life. Or my friend who swam against a rip current to save his mother from drowning. If he had just been thrown into that current and told to swim against it, he probably would have given up. But because he had a reason for suffering through that exhausting swim, he found the strength to reach deep inside himself and accomplish his goal.

The point is that we're all better at doing hard things when we know *why* we're doing them, and when that reason is important to us. We all discover inner reserves of strength, persistence, and courage when we know there's a diamond at the bottom of the hole, whether that diamond is a graduate degree, a successful weight-loss program, or a better relationship with an estranged sibling. I call this phenomenon "knowing your *why*," and I use it with my clients every day.

Why You Need a *Why*

If you have a straightforward goal in mind, like losing ten pounds or getting a promotion at work, you may be wondering why it's important to define that goal more clearly. Isn't it obvious why somebody would want to drop excess weight or get a higher salary? Yet over and over, I have found that clients with vague, fuzzy, generic goals are far more likely to give up on them than clients with highly specific and detailed goals. And clients who can *visualize* their goals do the best of all. Human beings are much more motivated by stories, images, and fantasies than they are by vague concepts. So when I'm working with clients who want to make big changes, the first thing we do is identify their goals, then define them in as much detail as possible. I make them tell me their *why*.

For example, I once worked with a client who was recovering from a major illness. She'd been bed-bound for three months and had recently been assigned a set of physiotherapy exercises to build up her strength and get her moving again. But her body was weak, her energy was low, and she felt depressed and hopeless. The exercises were exhausting and uncomfortable, and she didn't see enough progress day by day to stay motivated. She'd already tried strategies like putting a star on the calendar for each day she did them, and asking a friend to call and nag her every evening to make sure she did them. But neither of these methods was working. She felt guilty when she didn't do her exercises, but feeling guilty and feeling motivated are not the same thing. She needed a clear image in her mind to motivate her. She needed to focus on *why* her physiotherapy was important to her.

We spent a session talking about her life, trying to locate a powerful image that would not only incentivize her, but inspire her to commit to her physiotherapy in a deep way. We talked about her career, her marriage, and her love of gardening, but none of these topics held enough juice to overcome the aversion she had to the therapy. Then we got onto the topic of kids, and the energy of the conversation changed markedly. This client had a six-year-old son who was rambunctious and full of energy. Every day, he asked her for a piggyback ride. And each time he asked, she thought: "I can't do this." She was hardly strong enough to carry the groceries in from the car, let alone lift a seventy-pound boy onto her back.

I asked her to imagine herself giving her son the piggyback ride he wanted so badly. I asked her to imagine his smile, and her laughter, and the feeling of his warm body on her back as she carried him around the room. Before I knew it, she had started crying. "I think I just found my *why*," she said. From that day forward, whenever she was having a hard time getting motivated to do her therapy, she returned to this image and, no matter how tired she was feeling, it motivated her to get off the couch and do one set of exercises. Bit by bit, her strength returned, until, one day when her little boy made his request, she surprised him by crouching down and inviting him to climb onto her back, just as she'd been dreaming of for months.

Even though this client had hundreds of reasons for becoming active again, it was only when she located this powerful mental image that she became willing to face any discomfort and overcome any setbacks to achieve her goal. When she was unsure of her motivation, she lacked the perseverance required to push through difficulties. Once she located her *why*, it became easier to keep going, even in the face of disappointment and hardship. She realized the hurdles she faced were only that—hurdles to be leapt over, not insurmountable walls.

Another client recently went back to school to become a teacher. She was tired of the low wages she was earning as a teacher's assistant and looked forward to the higher income that would come with her degree. But this client *hated* being a college student. She didn't just hate it; she mortally despised it. The lectures, the homework, sitting in a chair all day when she was used to being on her feet working with kids all conspired to make every day a slog, and she seriously considered dropping out.

When I asked her to tell me *why* she wanted to complete her degree, she answered: "Adelfa, you already know my *why*. Teachers make three times as much as teaching assistants."

"I have a feeling that's not your real reason," I replied. "What picture comes into your mind when you think about being a teacher? Is it really a picture of a bigger paycheck, or is it something else?"

She thought about it for a moment, and then she looked at me in surprise. "No," she said. "When I think about being a teacher, what comes into my mind is the fantasy of going to a party and, when a stranger asks me what I do for a living, I say: 'Oh, I'm a teacher.' I imagine myself feeling pride and self-respect, knowing that I have this great career. When people ask me what I do, I want to feel proud of the answer."

"I think you just found your real *why*," I told her, and we both burst out laughing.

After that, whenever my client found herself sitting in a boring lecture or pushing through some difficult homework, she imagined herself at that party, telling a stranger that she was a teacher. She imagined the sense of pride she would feel, saying these words. This one little fantasy gave her the rocket fuel she needed to finish her degree.

Find Your *Why*

As you can see from this example, your own personal *why* may not be what you or anybody else expects. The truth is, you may be a person who is more motivated by pride than by money, or by love for others than by doing something for yourself. Sometimes the first couple of reasons you hit on for doing something are weak, because they come from your head, not from your heart. But the deeper you dig, the more you will uncover your strongest motivations—the ones that will keep you going when things get hard and propel you toward accomplishing your goals.

So instead of asking clients to tell me their biggest reason for doing something—which tends to put them into thinking mode and produce the most obvious, conventional answers—I like to ask them to close their eyes and tell me the first image that pops into their heads when they think about their goals. The results are always surprising.

You may see yourself standing on a mountaintop, or receiving your diploma, or embracing a long-lost friend. Your mental image doesn't have to be dramatic—a simple one will do just fine, if it carries powerful emotions for you. After you hit on a meaningful image, refine it even further, adding sensory detail and homing in on the emotions it carries. This image then becomes an incredible source of power, like a secret talisman you can use to give yourself strength when your goal feels unachievable.

When you are ready to find your *why*, start by asking yourself the following questions:

* When you imagine yourself achieving your goal, what image comes into your mind?

* Where are you located geographically when you envision achieving your goal?

* What are you wearing? What are you doing? Who are you with?

* How do you feel inside when you see yourself having achieved your goal?

Hold the image in your mind until you're confident you've absorbed every detail. If the first image that comes up feels forced, let your mind wander until a more honest one bubbles to the surface. In your deepest heart, what is most important to you about achieving your goal?

You can also brainstorm potential sources of motivation, writing down as many as you can think of, then circling the ones that feel most potent. Think about your favorite movie or novel heroine. What motivates her to undertake her great task? Here are some examples to get you started:

* Love

* Money

* Pride

* Service to others

* Righting a wrong

* Standing up for a dearly held belief or value

* Protecting your children

* Following a passion

Once you get in the habit of identifying motivations, it gets easier and easier. You may find yourself returning to your *why* multiple times over the course of a day, every time you feel tired, distracted, or lost. If you're like me, you may even find yourself identifying the *why* for small everyday tasks like washing the dishes (because I value the sense of peace I feel in a clean house), not just for your major goals. Knowing your *why* can imbue your whole life with greater purpose and meaning, and restore a sense of agency when you are pushing yourself to complete a difficult task.

Count Your Wins

A few years ago, I had a client who was struggling to leave an abusive relationship. Even though she had a really strong *why*, the process of leaving was taking longer than she thought it should, and she had started to beat herself up for being "too weak," "too confused," and "too incompetent" to carry out a plan. The problem here was not lack of motivation. She had no shortage of powerful reasons for leaving the relationship. The problem was an inability to see and value the many things she had already done to achieve her goal.

I asked her to look at what she'd written in her journal over the last three months, and to highlight every place where she'd written about something she'd done that would someday help her leave. For example, on one day, she wrote about opening her own separate bank account. On another, she wrote about researching apartments for rent in a different town. When we went through her journal together, we realized that, over the last three months, she had taken no fewer than *sixteen* concrete actions that would eventually help her leave the relationship. She wasn't weak, or confused, or incompetent. She had been working steadily to build a new life for herself. She just couldn't see it until she reviewed her journal.

From that point on, my client began a practice of "counting her wins." Whenever she took any step toward building her independence, no matter how tiny, she logged it in her journal. Every week, she reviewed these entries to remind herself of how much she was already doing to move toward her goal of leaving her abusive partner. This practice transformed the way she saw herself—from a powerless, ineffective person, to a strong, intelligent woman who could live her own life. Three months after starting this practice, she left her abusive relationship for good.

Sometimes you have a strong *why*, but still have trouble achieving your goal. You're only human after all. When you get tired, or sick, or overwhelmed, you can fall behind on your goals no matter how motivated you are. This is why I am passionate about teaching my clients to count their wins.

This is something I had to learn the hard way. I used to have such high expectations of myself that anything short of a massive victory felt insignificant. "After all, do we need to applaud fish for swimming?" I would say.

Then one evening, shortly after moving to California, my husband and I had some friends over for dinner. We had a new baby, and I was struggling with feelings of inadequacy and low self-worth. As my friend was leaving our home that evening, she stopped and looked at my soul through my eyes. "What you did isn't easy," she said. "Not everyone can leave home to start a new life with a new person the way you did, and at the age you did. I see you. I see all you do. You're a good mom, and you're a good fucking woman. Not many people can do what you did."

By the time my friend had uttered the words "isn't easy," I was already crying. It hit me like a ton of bricks to be seen and recognized in this way. Words mean a lot to me—hearing them, writing them, reading them—so to have her tell me I was doing okay had a powerful effect on my mental state. Because she's a person I respect and admire, I knew her words were sincere. She wasn't just fluffing me up; she really meant it.

The truth is that I *am* a wonderful and present mother. I also work hard and accomplish a lot. But I rarely stopped to acknowledge my own accomplishments, let alone to feel proud of them. Instead, I just kept pushing myself to do more, achieve more, succeed more, produce more, be more. When my friend told me she recognized all that I did, my internal hamster wheel stopped spinning for a second—and it was incredible. After that, I started a practice of counting my wins—the times when I opted in instead of opting out, or went the extra mile when I didn't have to. I've become a happier person as a result, and I love to share this practice with my clients.

No Win Too Small

How many people enjoy jobs or lifestyles in which it's possible to score massive victories every single day? Even professional sports players don't have that experience. Most of us work quietly month after month and, when victories come to us, they may not even be very significant to anyone else. That's why it's important to learn to appreciate the tiny wins in your life—the moments when you decide to act from your highest self, whether that's making your bed in the morning or getting your butt to night class when you'd rather stay home and watch TV.

The more you celebrate the small wins in your life, the more you realize how much you do in a day, how much you care, and how kind you are. You can even experiment with saying "thank you" to yourself. Like my client who was recently divorced and swamped with work, but still took the time to fold her clothes nicely and put them away so her future self could enjoy putting them on later. Ask yourself: "If a friend had done this for me, how would I respond?" Chances are, you'd shower the friend with gratitude for doing the same things you take for granted when you do them yourself. Taking good care of yourself is no small feat, and neither is taking care of your family, your living space, or the ordinary tasks of life. These things deserve to be counted and enjoyed.

A small win may be walking into a social situation without knowing exactly what you're going to say. It may be taking an intentional breath before agreeing to take on a new project at work. It may be sending a text you were nervous about, or asking a favor from somebody, or remembering to write in your journal before bed. It may be diving into a challenging project even when you have no idea how you're going to figure it out. Or it may be as simple as remembering to feed your dog and put clean water in his bowl.

If you're working with a specific goal, it can help to start by writing down every single win that relates to that goal, no matter how small it is. For example, if your goal is to lose weight, a small win might be: "I walked up the stairs instead of taking the elevator." Or: "I had a private dance party to unwind after work instead of having a snack." Or: "I spent five minutes visualizing my *why*." When you write down these small wins, you simultaneously learn to see yourself as a new person. If you are used to thinking of yourself as lazy, seeing your wins written down can help you see yourself as hard-working and committed. If you are used to thinking of yourself as sedentary, writing down your wins can help you take on a new identity as an active person—which increases the likelihood that you will be even more active!

When I was first getting started on social media, I posted a message about some bath products I love. Amid the likes and comments, there was one that sent me into a tailspin of anxiety and self-doubt. "Why can't you post about something cheaper for once," the person asked, "instead of luxe products that normal people can't afford?" As soon as I read this, I felt flustered and defensive. After all, I grew up in the projects. I've been working ever since I was fourteen years old. I *am* a normal person! I just like to save my money so I can buy nice things now and then.

I sat back and watched all these emotions walking right up to my inner doorbell camera and ringing the bell—outrage, defensiveness, self-righteousness, and even embarrassment. Did people really think I was some rich lady? Is that how the whole world saw me? I started to type back a quick response, but I caught myself and took an extremely deep, *suuuuper* intentional breath instead. "Good job, Adelfa," I congratulated myself. "You remembered to take that breath."

Even though I hadn't yet resolved the situation, I'd already racked up a tiny win, and I was going to fucking celebrate that win. And guess what? Celebrating that win set me up for even more wins, because it put me in a positive, creative mindset. I took a couple of moments to think, and to connect with my compassion for the person who had sent me spiraling. After a few minutes, I wrote a kind, honest, and dignified response, instead of the off-the-cuff reaction I could easily have banged out.

If you find yourself in a challenging situation, counting your wins can help you come back to your center and reconnect with your highest self. By acknowledging the good you're already doing, you set yourself up to do even more good. And that's a win for everybody.

Try This:

* Sometimes your *why* may change over time. This is totally normal and okay! For example, my client first got motivated to do physiotherapy so she could give her son a piggyback ride. But later, her motivation was to start working again. Check in with yourself to see if your former motivations are still the most accurate. If they're not, take some time to

come up with a new mental image to power you along.

* Use your journal to record your wins every day. Do you notice your self-image shifting in response to this new information?

* If you're in the middle of a conflict, an argument, or some other challenging situation, take a moment to appreciate one good thing you've already done to handle it. Notice how that changes your mood, and gives you the confidence to proceed.

Conclusion: This Sh*t Is Easier Than You Think

Have you ever known people who were so effortlessly kind and at ease that they made everyone around them feel a little bit better? People who make both friends and strangers feel seen and understood? People who never seem to be involved in any drama, even when hit with the same unavoidable disasters as the rest of us? Who are just a little bit more Zen than average, a little harder to knock off balance, a little more compassionate toward themselves and everyone around them?

Well, if you haven't, I have a feeling that you're going to meet one soon—because if you work with the tools in this book, that person is *you*.

Learning to observe yourself, gain distance from your reactions, and find emotional balance may be unfamiliar to you, but it doesn't have to be difficult. The techniques we've talked about here are not esoteric or complicated. And although they may take some courage, they require less effort than your usual patterns of resisting, distracting, and sticking to familiar habits. You heard me right.

Living a kind, compassionate, emotionally balanced life is *less* work than stumbling through life being hard on yourself and having no boundaries. Although life will continue to throw mountains of shit your way, when you use the tools in this book, you begin to realize that you are perfectly capable of handling it all.

You don't have to be perfect. You don't have to be in complete control of your own emotions, or anyone else's. You can trust in life and in your own integrity. When things go wrong, you can trust in your ability to take appropriate action. And when things go right, you can open yourself to experiencing your joy fully.

As a final thought, I want to remind you that doing the work to find emotional balance is not a selfish act. When you take a breath, set a boundary, count your wins, or do any other type of self-care practice, you are doing a service for everyone around you—your kids, your family, your coworkers, and your friends. As you become calmer and more at ease, you naturally extend these benefits to the people in your community. As you become kinder to yourself, you expand your capacity for kindness toward others. The more you lighten your own burden, the less conflict you bring to your relationships, and the more energy you free up for helping the less fortunate.

In other words, the goal of self-care is not just to make *you* feel better. It's to unleash your potential to heal the entire world. Whether that means becoming an activist, helping a friend in need, fostering animals, or restoring a habitat, establishing emotional balance in yourself sets you on a path to embodying your highest values and achieving your highest goals. So get out there and do whatever fills your *corazón*—whatever floods you with gratitude, lights your fire, fills your cup. I know you can do it, and I'll be rooting for you every step of the way.

Acknowledgments

I'm so glad these sections exist because I couldn't imagine going through this journey alone. To say I'm sitting in gratitude is a serious understatement, but until I find another easily digestible phrase, I'll just share my gratitude in the only way I know how—by word-vomiting my deep, loving emotions to those I love.

First, I don't think it would've been possible to complete this journey without my husband and son. Manny, my love, there aren't enough words to describe how grateful I am we found each other in this lifetime. From start to finish you've been supportive, encouraging, and generously patient with me. It's never lost on me how much of my successes and joy are attributed to you. I love you deeply. And my Umi, you are my sunrises and sunsets, baby boy. Life isn't life without you. My forever reason for being and my bestest of friends, te amo.

Thank you Hierophant Publishing and the hardworking team that helped make this book a reality. Randy, thank you for believing in this piece. To Hilary, Addie, Laurie, and Grace, thank you for the guidance, understanding, and patience to help grow this book into all it became, and a big thank you to Bud for bringing me in and getting this show on the road.

Another big thank you to the greatest friend, my Nads, who not only cheered me on but also read through this in many of its phases with pure love. Salud to my spirit team for creating this path and the many to come that'll be as joyous, loving, and fruitful. The Dizzles, I love you and thank you for cheering me on throughout this journey. Pamela, Chris, Jaki—my love for you runs deep, thank you.

The loving, caring, beautiful community that has formed due to this journey—thank you. Over the years your support, love, care, and trust has rippled onto these pages as well. There's a wealth of love for you in me.

Y dejo lo mejor para lo ultimo—mami y papi, como los quiero y les agradezco todo los que han hecho por mi. Por ser los mejores padres en este mundo y llenarme con amor y felicidad les quiero dar unas gracias immensa. Se que sin ustedes, no fuera la mujer ni la hija, ni la madre o esposa o amiga que soy hoy en dia. Los amo con todo mi alma y este corazoncito. Dame luz que hoy se bebe!

Endnotes

1. Lieberman, Matthew D., Naomi I. Eisenberger, Molly J. Crockett, Sabrina M. Tom, Jennifer H. Pfeifer, and Baldwin M. Way. "Putting Feelings into Words." *Association for Psychological Science* 18, no. 5 (May 2007): 421–28. https://doi.org/10.1111/j .1467-9280.2007.01916.x.

2. Schroder, Hans S., Tim P. Moran, and Jason S. Moser. "The Effect of Expressive Writing on the Error-Related Negativity Among Individuals with Chronic Worry." *Psychophysiology* 55, no. 2 (September 8, 2017). https://doi.org/10.1111/psyp.12990.

3. Dimitroff, Lynda J., Linda Sliwoski, Sue O'Brien, and Lynn W. Nichols. "Change Your Life Through Journaling: The Benefits of Journaling for Registered Nurses." *Journal of Nursing Education and Practice* 7, no. 2 (August 2017): 90–98. https://doi.org/10.5430/jnep .v7n2p90.

About the Author

Adelfa Marr is a life coach whose practice focuses on providing a safe, no-disclaimer space where clients can become the best version of themselves. She lives in Southern California with her husband, actor Manny Montana, and their son. Learn more about her at adelfamarr.com.

Also from Hierophant Publishing

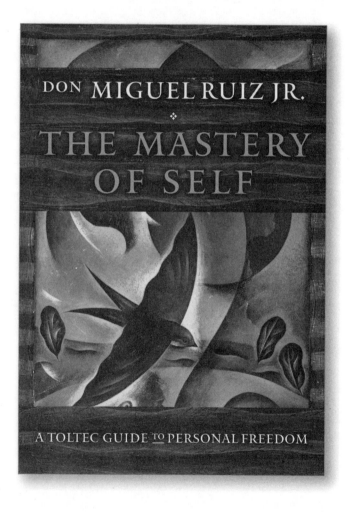

Available wherever books are sold.

Also from Hierophant Publishing

Available wherever books are sold.

San Antonio, TX
www.hierophantpublishing.com